Most Certainly True
LUTHERAN HISTORY AT A GLANCE

75 Stories About Lutherans Since 1517

Mark Granquist, editor

Lutheran University Press
Minneapolis, Minnesota

Most Certainly True
LUTHERAN HISTORY AT A GLANCE
75 Stories About Lutherans Since 1517

Mark Granquist, editor

Copyright © 2017 Lutheran University Press, an imprint of 1517 Media. All rights reserved. No part of this book may be reproduced or transmitted in any form by any means, electronic, mechanical, recording, or otherwise, without the express permission of the publisher. For information or permission for reprints or excerpts, please contact the publisher.

Many of these chapters were originally published in the Metro Lutheran as part of the Faithful and Reforming column. Used with permission.

ISBN-13: 978-1-942304-27-2
eISBN-13: 978-1-942304-69-2

Contents

Introduction 7
Table of Acronymns 14
1   Luther's Theological Legacy: Trusting Jesus Christ—Alone 15
2   The Ninety-Five Theses: All About Sin and Its Consequence ... 18
3   Philip Melanchthon: Enigmatic Reformer 21
4   The Augsburg Confession: Defense, Profession, and Invitation 24
5   Women Active in Luther's Reformation 27
6   Concordia: A Formula for Peace 30
7   Lutheran Hymns for Terrible Times 33
8   Rasmus Jensen: First Lutheran Pastor in North America 35
9   Slovak Lutherans: A Tough-minded People 38
10 Lutherans in the Caribbean 41
11 Spener and Pietism 44
12 Lutherans in the American South 47
13 Schwartz Reaches Out to India 50
14 From Salzburg to Georgia 53
15 Lutherans and Native Americans 56
16 Henry Melchior Muhlenberg: A Leader of American Lutherans 59
17 Colonial Lutheran Pastoral Care 62
18 Father Heyer: On the Move for the Lord 65
19 "Praise the Lord:" Lutherans and American Revivalism 68
20 Löhe: The Man Who Wouldn't Take No for an Answer 71
21 C. F. W. Walther:
    Founder of the Lutheran Church–Missouri Synod 74
22 When Is a Lutheran Not a Lutheran? 77
23 William A. Passavant: Gospel Ranger 80
24 The Apostolic Lutheran Tradition 83
25 Samuel Simon Schmucker and the General Synod 86
26 African-American Lutherans 89

27 Daniel Payne and Jehu Jones: African-Americans and Lutheranism 92
28 The Clash at Koshkonong: Eielsen and Dietrichson 95
29 Father Adam Keffer and Early Canadian Lutheranism 98
30 Elisabeth Fedde, Founder of Norwegian-American Lutheran Deaconesses 101
31 Danes Enriched the Mix 104
32 Education for Lutheran Children 107
33 American Lutherans and the Civil War 111
34 Lutherans in Madagascar 114
35 Theological Fights: The Question of Predestination 117
36 Germans from Russia in U.S. Lutheranism 120
37 Forgotten Giant: Johan Arndt Aasgaard 123
38 Preachers, Pietists, and Socialists: Finns in North America ... 126
39 The Lutheran Fraternal Phenomenon 129
40 Lutherans in Papua New Guinea 132
41 Icelandic Lutherans in North America 135
42 Colleges and Controversy: Augsburg and St. Olaf 138
43 Thea Rønning: One Life Among Many 141
44 Reindeer and Hunger and Hope: Brevig Mission and Shishmaref Lutheran Churches 144
45 Come to the WELS! Wisconsin Evangelical Lutheran Synod ... 147
46 Emmy Evald: A Vision for Women's Leadership 150
47 Bold Woman Day 153
48 Lutherans Go Latin: Hispanic Lutheranism 157
49 Richard Reusch: Cossack, Scholar, Missionary, Teacher, Pastor 160
50 Lutherans and the Lodge 163
51 Praising God in English: Lutherans and the Language Transition 165
52 Red and Green and Black and Blue: Lutheran Hymnals and Their Impact 168
53 Lutherans Learn to Cooperate 171
54 Evangelism: Lutherans and "the Boat" 174
55 American Lutherans Face War and Depression 177

56 The Last Voyage of the Zam Zam 180
57 American Lutheran Aid to Refugees 183
58 Courageous Journeys:
   Lutheran Immigration and Refugee Service 186
59 Lutherans from the Baltic 189
60 "The Church May Not Just Doze:" Confessing in Indonesia 192
61 The Story of Two Lutheran Mergers 195
62 Polity and Piety: The Association
   of Free Lutheran Congregations 198
63 Franklin Clark Fry: "Mr. Protestant" 201
64 "Out of Necessity:" The Church of the Lutheran Confession ... 204
65 Warren A. Quanbeck: Lutheran Ambassador-At-Large 207
66 A Mining Town Turns Lutheran 210
67 Lutherans Going Public: Should the Church Do Politics? 213
68 U.S. Lutherans as Selective Pacifists 216
69 Lutherans Seeking Social Change in Racist Alabama
   Half a Century Ago 219
70 August 1961: Martin Luther King and Lutherans Divided 222
71 Women's Ordination 225
72 Bread for the World: How Lutherans Have Led 228
73 For Lutherans, the Quintessential "Family Reunion" 231
74 The Newest Lutheran Denominations: LCMC and NALC 234
75 Wittenberg Meets Addis Ababa: Lutherans in East Africa 237
For Further Reading and Reference 240
Acknowledgments 242

Martin Luther statue in Wittenberg, Germany. The inscription on the book Luther is holding reads *"Bücher des Alten Testaments ENDE / Das Neue Testament verdeutscht von Doktor Martin Luther"* (Books of the Old Testament / The New Testament translated into German by Dr. Martin Luther).

Introduction

There are many ways to tell a story, and after 500 years of the Lutheran family, there are lots of stories to tell. For a movement that is so large and so old, the story of Lutheranism could be told in any number of large and important books—and if you are interested in such books, there's a list of them in the back of this volume. But sometimes, in trying to tell the big story, the smaller stories get lost. There are just so many details that readers can lose track about where they are and what is going on.

This book will try to tell the narrative a different way, by focusing on the small stories—the stories of Lutheran individuals and groups and events over the course of 500 years. Each one is brief, only about 800 words. But the stories themselves illustrate their particular time and place, and give you, the reader, a sense of how Lutherans lived out their faith in their particular context.

Hopefully, you will be inspired to do more reading after this book and to think about your life of faith and how you yourself might be called to act on God's mission in the world. Your calling may not be as dramatic as the stories presented here, but certainly your calling is as important as any of them. You might name the people in these stories "heroes," and perhaps they are. But if you live out God's calling where you are, you can be a hero to those who need your help and your presence in your place, in your time.

If you wish, you might want to know have an idea of the "big picture" before you read these stories. So the rest of this introduction will be the telling of 500 years of the Lutheran story in a very condensed version. You may wish to read this big story before the smaller stories, or you may wish to reverse the order—either way is fine.

500 Years of Lutherans, 1517-2017

The Lutheran family is the oldest and largest part of the Protestant section of the Christian faith (the other two sections being the Roman Catholic Church and the Orthodox churches). Martin Luther

(1483-1546) was a Catholic monk and priest in Germany who was deeply troubled by the abuses he saw in the churches of his day. In 1517 he began to publically protest against these abuses, and called for the reform of the medieval church. But the church was not ready for reform, because too many people were making too much money off things the way they were. Church leaders passionately opposed Luther; he was excommunicated from the church, and the Emperor put him under condemnation. But Luther's bold stand awakened many others across Europe, and the movement known as Protestantism began. Luther worried that the Gospel good-news of God's saving grace was being lost under the sheer weight of religious commands and "busy-ness." The new Protestant churches called themselves "Evangelicals," after the Greek word meaning "good news."

Luther translating the Bible into German, the language of the people

The Lutheran movement formally dates from 1530, when the Lutherans were asked by the Emperor to give an account of what they believed. They responded with a theological document known as the Augsburg Confession (in Latin, *Augustana*), which is the basic theological "constitution" of Lutherans worldwide. If you want to know whether a group is Lutheran, ask if it holds formally to this

TIMELINE

1517	1521	1530	1580	1618-48	1619	1638	1666
Martin Luther posts his 95 Theses	Luther defies the emperor and church at the Diet of Worms	Augsburg Confession presented— defined the Lutheran movement	Publication of the *Book of Concord*— the Lutheran "constitution"	Thirty Year's War in Germany— Lutheranism in peril	Danes in Hudson Bay— first Lutherans in North America	New Sweden on the Delaware first American Lutheran colony	Danish Lutheran church founded in the Virgin Islands

document. Further foundational documents were gathered together in 1580 in the Book of Concord (in Latin, *Concordia*). The Lutheran movement spread and was formally established in central and northern Germany, in Scandinavia, and in smaller pockets in Eastern Europe. Though there were terrible wars of religion in the sixteenth and seventeenth centuries between Catholics and Protestants (especially the Thirty-Years War, 1618-48), Lutheranism survived, and even flourished.

The Thirty Year's War devastated Europe.

In most of Europe, Lutherans formed territorial or "state" churches, meaning that all church in that country were Lutheran, and supported by the government (they did not believe in religious pluralism at all). Officially, all people in that particular country were Lutherans; to be a Swede or a Saxon was to be a Lutheran. This "establishment" of religion allowed for the Lutheran movement to solidify, but in time this situation led to a cooling of Lutheranism's original fervor and spirit. New voices arose calling for a renewal and reform of Lutheranism itself, including Philip Jakob Spener in his work *Pia Desideria* (1675). This new movement, called Pietism, focused on the religious and moral lives of individuals, calling to "awaken" them to a vibrant Christian life. Theological struggles over Pietism continued to develop over subsequent centuries, but the impulses generated by

1675	1703	1734	1748	1820	1826	1834
Spener's *Pia Desideria*—Lutheran Pietist movement	Justus Falckner—first Lutheran ordained in North America	Salzburg Lutheran refugees form a colony in Georgia	Muhlenberg forms the Pennsylvania Ministerium	Formation of the General Synod—first national organization	Gettysburg Seminary founded	St. Paul's Colored Lutheran congregation, Philadelphia, founded

this movement led to a new spirit of mission within Lutheranism, especially the spread of the gospel to North America, Asia, and Africa.

In the eighteenth century, European Lutherans were beginning to spread out into the wider world. They migrated to North America and founded settlements and congregations there, a movement that would later blossom into a massive immigration, 1840-1920.

Lutherans gathered for worship in the new land.

The situation in North America was so much different than in Europe; there were no Lutheran state churches to support the Lutherans, rather a situation of religious liberty and pluralism. If Lutherans in North America wanted their own congregations, they had to organize, run, and pay for them themselves. And since there were very few Lutheran pastors among them, they also had to raise up such leaders on their own. It was a difficult situation for these European immigrants, but in the long run this freedom allowed the Lutherans to grow and flourish on the North American continent.

Beyond forming congregations, Lutherans in North America also developed other institutions—regional and national synods (denominations), colleges and seminaries, hospitals and other social service agencies—all to meet the needs of a growing Lutheran population. More than this, these North American Lutherans had to figure out

TIMELINE

1841	1847	1853	1855	1860	1867	1870s-80s	1917-18
"Father" Heyer—first American Lutheran missionary to India	German Evangelical Lutheran Synod of Missouri formed	Norwegian Synod in America formed	Definite Synodical Platform—fight over "American Lutheranism"	Augustana Synod (Swedish) formed	Formation of the General Council (rival to General Synod)	Fight over the doctrine of Predestination	First World War—end of immigration, beginning of language transition

how to be Lutheran in a religiously pluralistic and English-language context, something that was new to Lutheranism as a whole. There were old theological debates brought from Europe, and new ones from North America, that in one way or another all dealt with the same question; "What does it mean to be Lutheran?" These are questions that still occupy Lutherans around the world, even after 500 years.

During this period in the nineteenth century, Lutheranism was truly becoming a world-wide movement. Lutheran missionaries from Europe and North America traveled to countries in Asia and Africa to spread the Good News, first to India and China, then to other areas. Eventually substantial Lutheran churches were founded throughout Asia and Sub-Saharan Africa; in some countries, like South Africa and Australia, there were immigrant European congregations, but in most places the Lutheran churches brought in local people who had been converted to Christianity. Eventually, and especially after the end of European colonialism (post-1945) these Asian and African (and eventually Latin American) Lutheran churches became full and autonomous members of the worldwide Lutheran family. The growth of these churches, especially in Africa, has been dramatic in last fifty years, and they

Augustana missionary Gustav Carlberg with students at The Lutheran Theological Seminary in China, 1940s

1918	1930	1950s	1958	1960	1962	1970
Formation of the National Lutheran Council —Lutheran coordinating body; United Lutheran Church in America formed	American Lutheran Church (1930-60) formed	Dramatic expansion and growth of American Lutheranism	Service Book and Hymnal ("red" hymnal)	American Lutheran Church (1960-88) formed	Lutheran Church in America formed	First women ordained by Lutherans in North America

have a passion for the gospel that is a lesson to learn for European and North American Lutherans.

In the twentieth century the Lutheran movement continued to grow and develop. In Europe the Lutherans were deeply affected by the upheaval and destruction brought on by two world wars, which challenged them both materially and spiritually. Growing secularism in Europe after 1945 meant that though the state churches were still established and supported, the hold that religious life and faith had on the European people was greatly diminished. With this European secularism, the Lutheran churches in Europe had to re-examine themselves and begin the necessary process of renewing themselves, thinking about what  the Gospel could mean now in a very different cultural situation. For Lutherans in North America, the twentieth century was a time of growth and maturity, as the churches founded by immigrants became full members of their societies. Lutheranism here grew and developed strongly, although that growth has been challenged toward the end of the century by cultural and religious forces not unlike those in Europe. North American Lutheranism, while still strong, faces new challenges internally and externally in the twenty-first century, and, as in Europe, must re-imagine how to communicate the gospel message to a rapidly changing world.

Lutherans in the global South (Africa, Asia, and Latin America)

TIMELINE

1973	1978	1985	1988	2001	2010	2017
Seminex walk-out in St. Louis —leads to Missouri Synod schism	Lutheran Book of Worship ("green" hymnal)	Evangelical Lutheran Church in Canada formed	Evangelical Lutheran Church in America formed	Lutheran Congregations in Mission for Christ formed	North American Lutheran Church formed	Lutheran churches in Africa surpass membership of Western Lutheran churches

have seen growth, and in some places, rapid growth into the twenty-first century. They have become fully autonomous churches, but are dealing with massive social and economic changes in their countries which has strained their resources to their limits. Their problems are quite the opposite of Lutherans in Europe and North America; they have seen often remarkable numbers of new Christians coming into their congregations, but never enough pastors and resources to deal with this growth, and often in the context of unstable governments and societies, and too often the hostility of their neighbors. The twentieth century has also seen the development of world-wide networks in which Lutherans work together for the common good and the welfare of all peoples. The Lutheran World Federation and the International Lutheran Council, as well as Lutheran relief and missionary organizations, attempt to bring world Lutherans together, as well as to unite them for the good of the world.

After 500 years, the Lutheran tradition of Christianity has become a major part of Christianity around the globe. When it is true to itself, it stands for the transformative power of the gospel good news of Jesus Christ, which works salvation through the grace of God. It also stands for this love of God to be made real in the lives of people though education, social service, and advocacy. This reforming movement, however, is always in need of reform itself, and the challenges of the twenty-first century and beyond will continue to drive Lutherans back to a rediscovery of their gospel roots and their historical traditions. What began as a movement for reform continues as a movement for further reform, yet holding fast to the essentials which brought it into being in the first place.

Faithful and reforming after 500 years. Martin Luther would be proud.

MARK GRANQUIST, EDITOR

Table of Acronyms

AELC (1976-1987)	Association of Evangelical Lutheran Congregations
AFLC (1962-)	Association of Free Lutheran Congregations
ALC (1930-1960)	American Lutheran Church
ALC (1960-1988)	American Lutheran Church
Augustana (1860-1962)	Augustana Evangelical Lutheran Church (name change 1948)
ELC (1917-1960)	Evangelical Lutheran Church (name change 1948)
ELCA (1988-)	Evangelical Lutheran Church in America
ELCIC (1985-)	Evangelical Lutheran Church in Canada
LCMC (2001-)	Lutheran Congregations in Mission for Christ
LCMS (1847-)	Lutheran Church-Missouri Synod (name change 1947)
LCUSA (1966-1988)	Lutheran Council in the USA (cooperative body)
LFC (1897-1963)	Lutheran Free Church
LWF (1947-)	Lutheran World Federation (cooperative body)
NALC (2009-)	North American Lutheran Church
ULCA (1918-1962)	United Lutheran Church in America
WCC (1948-)	World Council of Churches (ecumenical agency)
WELS (1892-)	Wisconsin Evangelical Lutheran Synod (name change 1959)

Luther's Theological Legacy: Trusting Jesus Christ—Alone

In December 1936, Martin Luther thought that his death was near and, in fact, he nearly did die. His territorial ruler, John the Constant of Saxony, had enlisted him to prepare a summary of Lutheran teaching in preparation for a possible church council. Luther delivered, as he had in the past, but not before suffering a serious heart attack during the writing. The product of his work that winter would eventually be included in the collection of the authoritative Lutheran confessional writings, the *Book of Concord* of 1580. Early on in this piece, he wrote:

Portrait of Martin Luther by Lucas Cranach the Elder

> Here is the first and chief article: That Jesus Christ, our God and Lord, "was handed over to death for our trespasses and was raised for our justification" (Romans 4:[25]); and he alone is the "Lamb of God who takes away the sin of the world" (John 1[:29]); and "the Lord has laid on him the iniquity of us all" (Isaiah 53[:6]); furthermore, "All have sinned," and "they are now justified without merit by his grace, through the redemption that is in Christ Jesus . . . by his blood" (Romans 3[:25]) (Smalcald Articles, Part II, Article 1, paragraphs 1-4).

Notice that Luther develops this "first and chief article" (doctrinally summarized by St. Paul's "justification" above) by simply weaving together four familiar Bible passages. This is a fitting method for Luther, for he had been a professor of Bible at the University of Wittenberg for much of the past quarter century—and he was convinced that these particular passages spoke for themselves, without any need for extensive commentary on his part.

But it had not always been that way. Early in his career, even after he had begun teaching, the Word of God had not been so clear to him. Indeed, as he read the Bible then, he heard its demands and its accusation more clearly than its promises or its consolation. It was only when he had learned—after much prayer, study, and experience—to distinguish between *law and gospel* that the Word of God came alive for him. For then he came to read the Bible as above all the book that brought him the gospel of Jesus Christ, which did not demand from him ever more and ever better works. Now the Word invited him only to hear and trust the promises of him who had died and risen again *for him*. The personal righteousness that he was helpless to produce on his own was God's gift to him in Jesus Christ. Luther would come to call this the "righteousness of faith."

This gift of Christ's righteousness, which Luther came to appreciate fully in about 1518, was too good to keep confined to a university classroom. The gospel as Luther had come to understand it would transform not only his own theology and life and that of his immediate followers, but the teaching and lives great numbers in the Christian church as well.

If men and women were free—in Jesus Christ—from any need to please God by their own efforts or activities, they were now free to express their faith in all manner of service to their neighbors. St. Paul had described this Christian ethic as "faith active in love" (Galatians 5:6). Luther would call it simply "vocation." By this he meant that the gospel of Jesus Christ calls (Latin, *vocatio*) people to trust the mercy of

Luther defending himself before the Diet of Worms

God for every temporal and eternal need; and they in turn are invited to recognize their ordinary settings in life as places and opportunities for sacrificial service to others (hence the English noun "vocation"). No longer were some works valued or esteemed more highly than others. This was true even of works that sixteenth-century church and society deemed as particularly "religious." Instead, the daily and routine tasks of life are perhaps even more important. Why? Because God has no need for human works, but the flesh-and-blood neighbor in need certainly does. Luther himself pulled these thoughts together beautifully in his Large Catechism of 1529:

> How could you be more blessed or lead a holier life, as far as works are concerned? In God's sight it is actually faith that makes a person holy; it alone serves God, while our works serve people. Here you have every blessing, protection, and shelter under the Lord, and, what is more, a joyful conscience and a gracious God who will reward you a hundredfold (Explanation of the Fourth Commandment, paragraphs 146-148).

The published writings of Martin Luther number literally thousands of pages. But the core of his thought can be captured in the conviction that Jesus Christ is a "mirror of the Father's heart." To know and be embraced by the love of God in Jesus Christ is the single greatest gift one can ever receive. It is Martin Luther's theological legacy that he unpacked that gift—its meaning and its implications—for his students and his parishioners. Thus he has passed it on to all those who trust Jesus Christ today.

DAVID A. LUMPP

The Ninety-Five Theses: All About Sin and Its Consequence

Martin Luther spent his career as a teacher of the Bible at the University of Wittenberg. However, when he assumed that role upon the completion of his doctor's degree in 1512, he did not give up his priestly and pastoral duties. He continued to preach frequently, and—most importantly for the topic of this article—he continued to hear the confessions of the men and women of his town parish. It was his experiences in this latter role that led him to prepare and post the Ninety-Five Theses on October 31, 1517, the day that has come to signal the beginning of the Lutheran Reformation.

Luther nailing the Ninety-five Theses to the Wittenberg church door

The tradition of seeing these theses as the dawn of the Reformation is somewhat misleading, for the theses themselves were neither a manifesto against the established Roman church nor a call to begin anything like a new church. Rather, the theses were a pastor-professor's carefully crafted call to an academic debate (e.g., they were written in Latin) about a subject with very practical consequences for his parishioners. Specifically, how were fallen people to deal with their sin—its presence in their lives, the guilt it causes, and the consequences to which it leads?

The Roman church of Luther's era dealt with those issues through its sacrament of penance, which entailed sorrow over one's sin (or "contrition"), oral "confession" of the sin(s), remission of one's eternal punishment, and then a prescribed act of "satisfaction" to deal with the remaining temporal consequences of the sin, which could be addressed either in this life or in purgatory (hence the expression "do penance"). This was further complicated at the time by the presence of "indulgences," which pertained to the "satisfaction" part of penance and amounted to a financial substitution for a performance penalty.

What Martin Luther had come to learn in the confessional was that pious people were burdened by sin and guilt, but they were finding false consolation in the purchase of these "indulgences." The traditional Roman sacrament of penance no longer squared with what Luther had learned in his study and teaching of the Bible, and this was especially true of the way it was being practiced in the months leading up to October 31, 1517. Hence, the Ninety-Five Theses are an indication of the problems Luther was experiencing in his pastoral work as well as the beginnings of a fresh and radically new approach to the Christian life.

Johannes Tetzel selling indulgences for the Roman church

First, Luther chose the word "repent" to describe what really ought to be going on here. "Penance" risked focusing more on human works than on God's once-and-for-all work in Jesus Christ. This is Luther's key point: Repentance is not about any human activity (not even one's sorrow or confession, much less one's act of "satisfaction"). In this sense, it is easier than all of that. One does not have to perform or purchase one's way into God's favor. Luther wrote: "Any truly repentant Christian has a right to full remission of penalty and guilt, even without indulgence letters. Any true Christian, whether living or dead, participates in all the blessings of Christ and the church; and this is granted him by God, even without indulgence letters" (theses 36 and 37). In short, focus on the Word of God. Focus on God's promise of full and free forgiveness in Jesus Christ.

Second, even if one does not need to earn or buy God's grace, Luther recognized that this approach to the Christian life (i.e., "perform these works of merit," or "procure this indulgence") was entirely inadequate, especially when one put his or her confidence in the works or the indulgences. Luther's study of the Scriptures taught him that the Christian life was much harder than Rome's sacrament of penance could lead one to assure. Indeed, he began the Ninety-Five Theses with this bracing observation: "When our Lord and Master Jesus Christ said `Repent' [Matthew 4:17], he willed the *entire life* of believers to be one of repentance" (thesis 1, emphasis added). He applied this to the immediate issue at hand a bit later: "Christians are to be taught that papal indulgences are useful only if they do not put their trust in them, but very harmful if they lose their fear of God because of them" (thesis 49).

A placard showing the Ninety-five Theses, from Luther's time

Yet if one does not have to follow sixteenth-century Rome's prescription for dealing with sin, and if that or any other works-oriented approach is inadequate anyway, what is one to do? Martin Luther would spend the rest of his career as a reformer fleshing out—and confessing—his answer to that question. It would go something like this: "For the sake of Jesus Christ, your sins are forgiven. Rely on this unconditional promise. Work now for others not because you are compelled to, but because you are freed and empowered to. In short, trust Jesus Christ and what he has done." While not all of this answer is present in so many words in the Ninety-Five Theses, what one does find there is an indispensable early expression of the theology of grace and of the cross that made it possible. Luther intimated as much in thesis 62, which provides a fitting summary of the entire document: "The true treasure of the church is the most holy gospel of the glory and grace of God."

DAVID A. LUMPP

Philip Melanchthon: Enigmatic Reformer

Lutheran Christians familiar with the basic tenets of their faith are sometimes surprised to learn that the person who formulated these truths in their most classical and "official" form was often not Martin Luther, but rather his friend, colleague, and, above all, co-confessor Philip Melanchthon.

Philip Melanchthon came to the University of Wittenberg primarily to teach Greek, but his intellectual breadth, rhetorical abilities, and pedagogical skills could never be confined to one area of study. Indeed, Philip was so gifted and influential that history has lauded him as the "teacher of Germany."

Though he taught at least two generations of students at Wittenberg, today the focus is usually on the substance of his teaching, as this is reflected in his most important writings. As a scholar who came to share—and even influence—Martin Luther's understanding of the gospel, Philip Melanchthon was the author of both the Augsburg Confession (1530), the defining confession of the Lutheran movement; and its Apology (1531), or Defense, which offers a thorough evangelical and biblical argument for the most basic proposals for doctrine and practice that had been made by Luther and his Wittenberg colleagues.

Philip Melanchthon

Especially in these writings, one discovers the classical Lutheran formulation of "justification"—that is, God pronouncing helpless sinners righteous—by grace alone, for Christ's sake alone, through faith alone. Melanchthon also insisted that it is necessary to distinguish carefully between God's accusing law and God's promissory gospel, and that this distinction is key to a proper interpretation and salutary reading of the Bible. Virtually everything else in these Lutheran confessional writings contributes to or derives from these two pervasive and interdependent themes, namely, the centrality of justification and the proper distinction between law and gospel.

In addition to many other academic and theological writings and a massive correspondence with some of the most important theological figures of the age, Melanchthon is best known for several editions of the first systematic textbook of Lutheran teaching, roughly translated as "Common Topics of Theology," the first edition of which in 1521 was lavishly extolled by Martin Luther.

But Philip's career was not without its share of controversy. Where Luther could sometimes be defiant, Philip was by personality irenic and conciliatory. As one who stood squarely in the middle of an unprecedented situation in Western Christendom, and who lived another fourteen years after the death of Luther himself in 1546, Philip faced a convergence of theological, political, and even military challenges that no one had confronted before. In an attempt to retain the gains of the Lutheran Reformation—and for Melanchthon nothing less than the restored preaching of the gospel of Jesus Christ itself was at stake—Philip put his considerable talents to work in an ongoing effort to find language that conflicting parties to various theological disputes would find acceptable. In the process, he won few friends, alienated some former students, experienced great personal frustration, and ensured that his own positions on these topics would be debated for the next 450 years.

Melanchthon's house in Wittenberg

Melanchthon's struggles to draft passable theological formulae did not involve insignificant topics. In revisions to the Augsburg Confession itself and in later editions of his theology textbook, his language led to renewed intra-Lutheran controversy on such major issues as the real presence of the body and blood of Christ in the Lord's Supper, the nature of conversion, the sense in which good works are necessary, and, when taken together, the doctrine of justification itself—which had been the centerpiece of both the Augsburg Confession and the Apology. To some, this Philip was a conciliator and almost prototypical ecumenist. To others, he was a once great figure who had compromised on the essentials of biblical truth itself.

Debates about Melanchthon's precise views on these and other controversial topics cannot be resolved here. However, scholarship of the past generation or two has been more generous and charitable in its overall assessment. For one thing, Philip was thrust often unwillingly into a convergence of historical circumstances that did not permit academic detachment or much abstract theological reflection. The very survival of the movement Martin Luther had initiated was at stake, and Philip sought to retain and quite literally hold together whatever he could, and to do so with theological integrity. In general, even those who remain critical of the substance of his later work are able to sympathize with the position he was in and to affirm at least the intent of his labors.

Certainly the best way to remember Philip Melanchthon is to recall him at his finest hour, as the scholar who was willing to stand before princes, an emperor, and theological opponents at Augsburg in 1530 and 1531 and produce some of the finest theological work to appear in two millennia of Christian history. In these writings, he affirmed over and over again that to know Jesus Christ is to know his blessings, "the promises which by the gospel he has spread throughout the world" (Apology of the Augsburg Confession, IV, 101).

DAVID A. LUMPP

The Augsburg Confession: Defense, Profession, and Invitation

June 25, 1530, was an auspicious day for the Christian church in the Holy Roman Empire, for on that day Saxon chancellor Christian Beyer read the Augsburg Confession to Emperor Charles V himself and to the other assembled representatives at the Diet of Augsburg in southwestern Germany. Prepared by Martin Luther's friend Philip Melanchthon, with input and background materials from other University of Wittenberg colleagues, the presentation of the Augsburg Confession on this day would come to be regarded as the "birthday" of the Lutheran church. In fact, this public confession has been so central to Lutheran identity that its adherents have often been referred to as the "Church of the Augsburg Confession."

The Diet of Augsburg

While immediate preparation for Augsburg can be said to go back a year or two from 1530, in many ways the Augsburg Confession was almost thirteen years in the making, ever since Luther had initiated the Reformation as a public movement with the posting of his Ninety-Five Theses in 1517. Teachers and leaders of the church were openly challenging some of the most important practices of the late medieval Roman church and, even more significantly, the theology on which those practices were based.

Simply stated, neither this Wittenberg appeal for reform nor the Roman disciplinary responses to it since 1517 had been successful. Followers of Luther hoped that the Diet of Augsburg in 1530 would demonstrate the validity of their critique and the strength of their evangelical theological claims. On the other hand, Rome sought the kind of rejection of the reformers' dissent that would curtail the spread of this movement once and for all.

As intriguing as the background historical detail is, much more important is the theological substance of the Augsburg Confession itself. As Luther had consistently done, Melanchthon begins by affirming the classical understanding of God as Holy Trinity, and the person of Jesus Christ as fully God and fully human, on which the consensus of the universal church had always been predicated. From there, he spells out what is absolutely central to the Reformation theological argument, namely, how Father, Son, and Holy Spirit forgive sinful humanity and restore spiritually helpless people to their created status as God's own daughters and sons. This gospel is classically encapsulated in the Confession's Article IV, on "Justification": "[W]e receive forgiveness of sin and become righteous before God out of grace, for Christ's sake through faith when we believe that Christ has suffered for us and that for his sake our sin is forgiven and righteousness and eternal life are given to us." Literally everything else in the twenty-eight articles of the confession points to, reasserts, or flows out of this article.

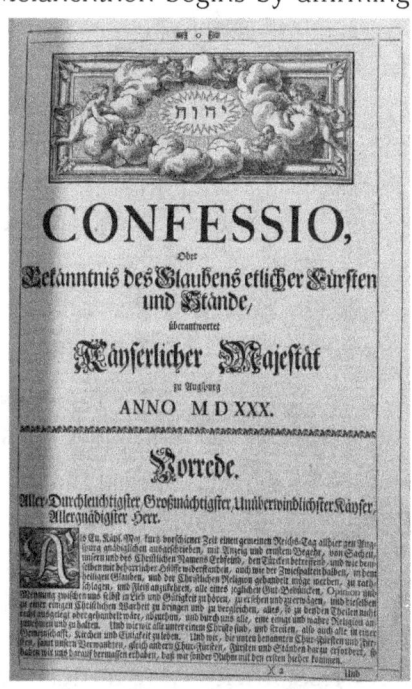

The Augsburg Confession, 1720

To offer but one example of each, the Augsburg Confession's discussion of human beings' fallenness underscores their inability to contribute in even the slightest way to their reconciliation with God. Indeed, they "cannot by nature possess true fear of God and true faith in God" (Article II, paragraph 1). These are not matters of personal decision or human achievement. For human beings to fear, love, and trust God requires the "grace, help, and operation of the Holy Spirit" (Article XVIII, paragraph 2).

The confessions' articles that are joined most directly to justification reiterate Article IV's point in similar language. The Christian life is not about earning favor with God; rather, "forgiveness of sins and justification are taken hold of by faith" (Article VI, paragraph 2). To assert anything else, Melanchthon never tires of repeating, actually minimizes and insults the work of Jesus himself.

The topics that emanate from justification are equally evangelical in character. The sacraments of Baptism and the Lord's Supper at their core are "signs and testimonies of God's will toward us in order thereby to awaken and strengthen our faith" (Article XIII, paragraph 1). Likewise, the church is defined not as an institution but in terms of the people whom God has restored through these very means of grace: "[The church] is the assembly of all believers among whom the gospel is purely preached and the holy sacraments are administered according to the gospel" (Article VII, paragraph 1).

These all too brief samples represent the theological core of the Augsburg Confession. The confession defended the changes in practice brought about by Luther's Reformation. It proposed a theological foundation and rationale for those reforms. In the process, the confessors at Augsburg were inviting their Roman contemporaries—and anyone else who would listen—to reexamine the Word of God and the ancient creedal tradition to determine for themselves whether or not these articles were a more faithful statement and elaboration of the gospel of Jesus Christ.

The invitation grounded in the Augsburg Confession's profession of faith has had a varied reception since that early summer afternoon in 1530. Today, Philip Melanchthon and his colleagues would doubtless be heartened that the confession they made over 480 years ago continues to be regarded as both abidingly valid and compelling. Above all, though, they would invite their fellow confessors of the twenty-first century to remain focused on God's unwavering promises in Jesus Christ, because these promises of forgiveness and new life are the point from which all Christian confessing truly begins and to which it all necessarily returns.

DAVID A. LUMPP

Women Active in Luther's Reformation

Women who were a part of and leaders in Luther's Reformation are often forgotten. While considerable attention has been given to Katie Luther, Martin's estimable wife, other significant figures have been overlooked. A brief glance at three women is illustrative of the varying ways they contributed to Luther's Reformation.

Elisabeth Cruciger (1500?-1535) was married to Casper Cruciger (1504-1548), one of Luther's colleagues on the faculty at Wittenberg. Born Elisabeth von Meseritz, she became a nun in Treptow, Pomerania, but fled from the convent to Wittenberg in the early 1520s. Cruciger was the first female Lutheran hymnwriter. Her hymn, "Herr Christ der einig Gottes Sohn" (Lord Christ, the Only Son of God) was published in the first evangelical hymnals, including the *Erfurt Enchiridion* (1524). Luther is reported to have praised it. It was translated into both Swedish and Danish in the 1520s. Translated into English, it was included in Miles Coverdale's hymnal *Goostly psalmes* (c. 1535). The hymn has a long history in Lutheran hymnals in Europe and North America and still occurs in many hymnals today. (*Evangelical Lutheran Worship* 309 and *Lutheran Service Book* 402, "The Only Son from Heaven," are shortened versions of the hymn.)

Katherine Von Bora Luther

Elisabeth Cruciger

Ursula of Münsterberg, granddaughter of the king of Bohemia, was born in the early 1490s. Her parents died while she was young, and she was placed in the convent of Mary Magdalene the Penitent in Freiberg. In the 1520s Luther's ideas influenced Ursula and other nuns. Ursula's statement of reasons for leaving the convent, addressed to Dukes George and Heinrich (her cousins), is dated April 28, 1528, some months before she actually left. She gave theological and personal grounds for her actions. She was convinced that salvation was by faith alone and found monastic life opposed to this. Showing a keen understanding of Luther's theology and its implications for her life, she complained of lack of access to the Word of God, being forced to receive the Lord's Supper when she was not ready, and a lack of opportunity to serve others as Christ commanded. Ursula left the convent on October 6, 1528, accompanied by two other nuns. They arrived in Wittenberg later that month and Luther took them in. Ursula asked Elector John for protection and, for the reasons for her flight, pointed to what she had written earlier. Ursula's defense, with an afterword by Luther, was printed in Wittenberg (twice) in 1528 and in Nuremberg (once) in 1529. In his afterword Luther noted that he had chosen to publish this account in order to praise the activity of God's Word in winning over people of low and high estate. While the date and place of Ursula's death are unknown, it is known that other nuns from Freiberg followed her example and left the convent, despite strict preventative steps. (Ursula's statement is found in *Convents Confront the Reformation: Catholic and Protestant Nuns in Germany* (1996). Luther's afterword is found in *Luther's Works*, volume 58).

Ursula of Münsterberg

Elisabeth, Duchess of Braunschweig-Lüneberg (1510-1558) had a lasting impact as both a ruler and a writer. Married at age fifteen to a man forty years her elder, Duke Erich of Calenberg- Göttingen, she bore four children. Through the influences of her mother, who converted to evangelical faith in 1528, her correspondence with Martin Luther, and her acquaintance with Lutheran pastor Antonius Corvinus, Elisabeth confessed her evangelical faith openly in 1538. Her husband remained Roman Catholic but did not hinder his wife in the exercise of her faith. After Erich died in 1540 and Elisabeth became regent for her minor son, she began to introduce the Reformation in her territories. Elisabeth thereby helped lay the foundation for what later became the Hannoverian territorial church, now one of the largest Lutheran churches in the world. She wrote the introduction to the church ordinance (1542) for her territories, making clear that her concern was that God's Word be preached clearly and purely. The church ordinance set up structures for education (including catechism for the laity), regulated worship practice (including communion in both kinds), and mandated all teaching be in accordance with the Augsburg Confession. Elisabeth's efforts bore fruit as her territories resisted subsequent attempts at recatholisation. Known as one of the most prolific female writers of the sixteenth century, Elisabeth wrote, among other works, a treatise for her son on the responsibilities of a prince and a book of consolations for women who had been widowed. In all her works, Elisabeth showed herself to be a thoughtful and forthright theologian.

Elisabeth, Duchess of Braunschweig-Lüneberg

While continuing to recognize the importance of the person and insights of Martin Luther, historians have increasingly focused on the men and women who supported and furthered Luther's Reformation in diverse ways. These three women were among many who understood their Christian faith in accordance with Luther's insights, publicly confessed that faith, and aided the progress of the Reformation.

MARY JANE HAEMIG

Concordia: A Formula for Peace

Most religious movements are initially focused on a particular individual, a visionary and inspiring leader around whom people can gather. It certainly was that way for the Lutheran movement in the sixteenth century; it was a theological movement gathered around the ideas of Martin Luther, and he was the one who gave it direction and purpose. (Even if he'd have preferred that it not be named after him!) Luther was much more than just Lutheranism's originator; during his long career he trained hundreds of its pastors and theologians, and served as the arbiter of its theological debates. It was his personal leadership that established this reforming movement in Germany and Scandinavia, and his ideas radiated much farther.

Yet, Luther could not live forever, and his death in 1546 came at a very critical time for the new reforming movement. Yes, the Lutheran (or Evangelical) churches were beginning to be established in Europe, supported by the German and Scandinavian countries, but in addition the counter-pressure from the papacy and the Holy Roman Empire was intensifying. The imperial (Catholic) forces were finally

An engraving showing the scene of Luther's death, titled "Victory in Death"

being turned against the new Protestants, and in 1547, the year after Luther's death, the imperial forces decisively defeated the Protestant forces in Germany. This defeat smashed the Protestant alliance and left the Lutherans weak and open to the forced imposition of papal authority in the Protestant territories in Germany.

Worse than this, after Luther's death the Lutherans were internally divided, and there was no one to take Luther's position of leadership. Luther's colleague, Philip Melanchthon, was not forceful in dealing with the Imperial threat, and was identified with one of the two theological parties within Lutheranism that had developed during the 1540s. The so-called "Philippists" were those who sought to compromise with the Catholics and make the best of the situation. They were also (some thought) too close theologically to the other Protestant group, the Reformed (or Calvinists). The second Lutheran group, the so-called "Gnesio" (old) Lutherans saw themselves as the true heirs of Martin Luther and urged stiff resistance against the Catholic forces, politically and theologically. It was a very dangerous time for the Lutherans to be leaderless and divided.

However, as often happens, the situation was soon reversed. Protestant forces turned back imperial forces, and with the Peace of Augsburg in 1555 the Lutherans were finally granted legal political status within the Holy Roman Empire. This peace gave the Lutherans some breathing room, politically and militarily, but it did not solve the internal theological problems within Lutheranism. In fact, the peace of Augsburg actually intensified these theological battles; with the external (military) threat eased, the need for unity was lessened, and theologians began debates that threatened to tear Lutheranism apart. On top of this, many of the Gnesio Lutherans had suffered personally from their stiff resistance to the Catholic forces, and they deeply resented the Philippists for their alleged "collusion" with the Catholic and Imperial authorities.

The theological battles between the two parties centered on issues such as justification, good works, sin, the nature of the human person, and other similar matter. But more deeply, it was a question of which group would define and direct the legacy of Luther, now that he was gone. One problem was Luther himself, who had written a huge amount of theological works over nearly thirty years, and not always consistently. Both sides could find many passages in Luther's writing that could be made to support their own claims.

It was left to a number of moderate Lutheran theologians to attempt to find a middle ground between the two warring parties, and to develop theological compromise. Led by Jacob Andreae, Nicolas Selnecker, David Chytraeus, Martin Chemnitz, and others, this moderate groups labored through the 1560s and 1570s to forge a document that would achieve theological peace, and define Lutheranism. In 1577 they accomplished their goal in a document entitled the "Formula of Concord," which carefully laid out the boundaries of Lutheran theology and practice; it was accepted and signed by over eight thousand Lutheran leaders in Germany. In 1580 this document, along with seven other documents, were gathered into the *Book of Concord*, which is the "constitution" of Lutheranism. Concord means "peace;" in Latin it is "*concordia*."

Jacob Andreae

Nicolas Selnecker

The Formula of Concord can be a tough document, and some do not like it for its harsh language against the Catholics and other Protestants. But it was written at a tough time, when Lutheranism was under siege from outside and facing dangerous dissention from within, and the Formula needed to clearly define Lutheranism in the midst of these problems. The Formula of Concord has continued to serve Lutheranism well over almost 450 years. It does not always solve theological issues, but it does define the boundaries of how theological debates should be carried out. Concord, indeed.

David Chytraeus

MARK GRANQUIST

Martin Chemnitz

Lutheran Hymns for Terrible Times

Lutherans have a unique history when it comes to hymns. Although a visit to some of our congregations might make one wonder whether the nickname is any longer justified, the original Lutherans, from 1517 forward, really did become a "singing church."

Martin Luther wrote some of the first hymns for the Lutheran movement. "A Mighty Fortress" has been called the Battle Hymn of the Reformation. And the solid hymnody that came to be known as the Lutheran chorale made it clear to those both within and beyond the Lutheran church that this denomination affirmed solid, biblically-grounded, God-centered texts and rugged, durable melodies.

A unique chapter in the history of Lutheran hymnody was written during one of the most frightening periods in the history of the church. By the early seventeenth century, Roman Catholic Church leaders—as well as military captains—thought they saw their chance to exterminate Lutheranism once and for all. They launched a bloody campaign designed to force Lutheran congregations back into the Roman fold. The battle raged primarily in Germany, between 1618 and 1648—hence, its name, the Thirty Years' War.

It is is hard to exaggerate the damage this bloody conflict did to Germany. Fully one-third of the German population was exterminated. Roman Catholic armies threatened for a period to win the day. In its darkest hour, Lutheranism was rescued by a Swedish army under the leadership of its Lutheran king, Gustavus Adolphus. (The Minnesota college with his name has a bronze bust of Gustavus on display on its campus mall.)

Many powerful Lutheran hymns of faith were created during this terrible time. One of the most famous, and most enduring, is one that Lutherans and other Christians often sing as though it were intended for use in happy times. In fact, Pastor Martin Rinkart's "Now Thank We All Our God" was set down on paper during a time of terror.

His city, Eilenberg (near Martin Luther's birthplace and death-city, Eisleben), fell under siege from invading armies. A pestilence ravaged the town, and famine killed many that disease did not. During this dark period Rinkart conducted funerals for nearly 5,000 people, including that of his own wife. In the midst of it all, he wrote "Now Thank We All Our God." (Contrary to what some believe, the hymn was not written to celebrate the end of the war; it was completed years earlier, in the midst of the fighting.)

Other notable Lutheran hymn writers from this period include Johann Heermann and Johann Crueger. Heermann wrote the text for "Ah, Holy Jesus, How Hast Thou Offended?" while Crueger composed the melody.

Johann Michael Altenburg wrote "Fear Not, Thou Faithful Christian Flock," considered by some musicologists to be one of the greatest hymns of Christian hymnody. During the war years Altenburg served a congregation near Erfurt, where Martin Luther once attended university. Altenburg's congregation lost 600 members due to wartime plague.

Johann Rist, who experienced the plundering of his home and loss of most of his possessions in 1643 while serving a Lutheran congregation near Hamburg, still managed to compose 659 hymns, two of the most familiar of which are "Break Forth, O Beauteous, Heavenly Light" and "O Living Bread from Heaven."

It has said that the Thirty Years War was a crucible in which Lutheranism was tested and found durable. Historians find high irony in the reality that, when the fighting ended with the Peace of Westphalia, the territories that each faith group—Lutherans and Roman Catholics—controlled were essentially the same as those they had possessed at the outset of the war. The boundaries didn't change much, but Germany was crippled economically or politically for generations. (Many in the first great wave of Lutheran immigrants coming to the U.S. left their ruined farms, shops, and homes following this war and migrated to Pennsylvania and adjoining states.)

The sources of Lutheran hymnody are diverse. Modern Lutheran hymnals contain far more than solid German hymns (including Scandinavian, English, African, and Latin American hymns). But the unique circumstances of the Thirty Years' War provided some of the most dearly bought and, for some, the most beloved hymnody in Lutheranism's musical treasury.

MICHAEL L. SHERER

Rasmus Jensen: First Lutheran Pastor in North America

He thought he was going to India. He wasn't even supposed to be in North America, but he ended up dying there and never did make it to Asia. But one thing makes us remember the name of Rasmus Jensen, the very first Lutheran pastor in North America.

King Christian IV of Denmark

In the seventeenth century, all the European nations were establishing trading posts in Asia, and King Christian IV of Denmark wanted to do so as well. So in 1619 the king sent out two expeditions to India. One traveled the usual route around the southern tip of Africa, establishing a Danish colony in India. The other, under the command of an adventurer and explorer, Jens Munk, went the other way, trying to force its way through the legendary Northwest Passage. It was believed back then that you could sail between Greenland and Canada, across the Arctic, and into the Pacific, in a shortcut to the riches of India, China, and Japan.

Among his crew, Munk was assigned a young Lutheran pastor named Rasmus Jensen. Jensen had studied at the University of Copenhagen and was appointed by the king to be a "ship pastor to the East Indies," in charge of the spiritual life and condition of the expedition itself and to the Danish colony in India once he had arrived. He was promised a salary of 100 dollars a year.

The Munk expedition through the Northwest Passage was neither the first nor the last of such attempts, but it did share one thing in common with the rest—it ended in tragedy. Munk's ships sailed

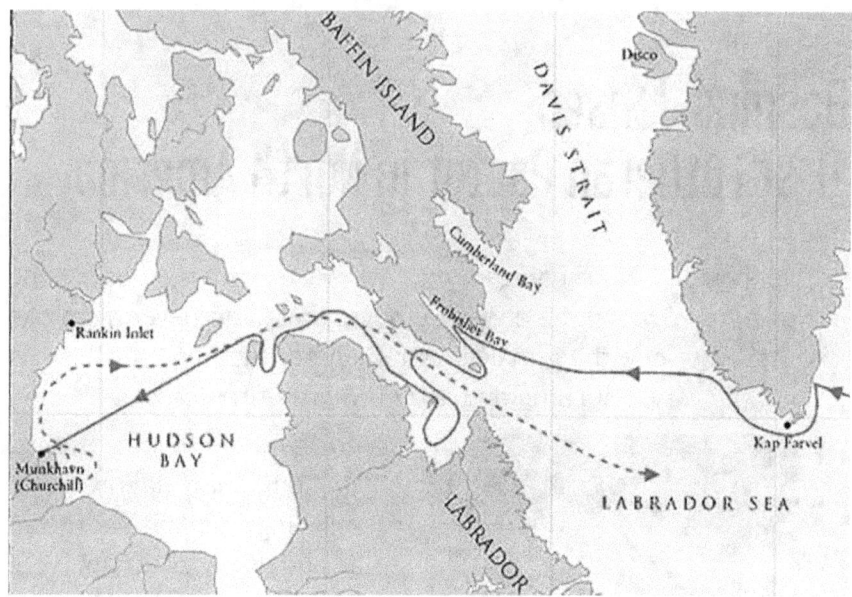

Route of the Jens Munk expedition

into the Canadian Arctic regions in the summer of 1619, entering Hudson Bay in August. But despite their constant attempts to do so, they could not find a suitable water route to the riches of Asia. In late September, with the Arctic winter quickly upon them, Munk made the fateful decision to spend the winter in Hudson Bay, hoping to find the fabled route west the next spring. They moored their ships near the present town of Churchill, Manitoba.

Initially, the winter was not too bad. The holidays of the Christian year were regularly celebrated, including St. Martin's Day on November 10, in honor of the fourth century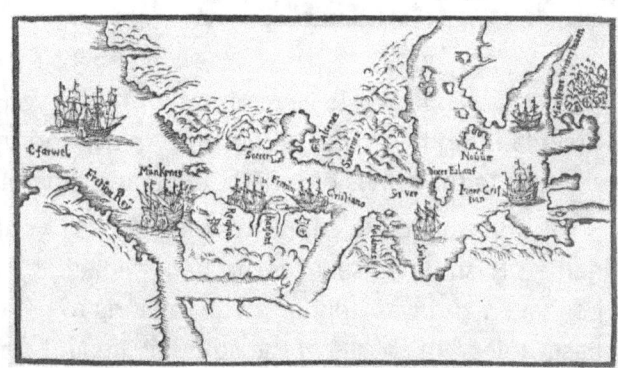

Jens Munk's hand-drawn map of their journey

saint and his namesake, Martin Luther. At Christmas time Pastor Jensen celebrated the customary religious services in the traditional liturgy of the Church of Denmark. Captain Munk recorded the following entry: "The Holy Christmas Day we all celebrated and observed solemnly, as a Christian's duty is. We had a sermon and chanting, and after the sermon we gave the pastor an offering, according to the ancient custom. . . ." Since they did not have money, they gave Pastor Jenson white fox skins.

Those fox skins came just in time, as the winter suddenly turned frigid with the New Year. The expedition was short on food and supplies, and their health began to decline rapidly. Before Christmas Pastor Jensen had already presided over the funerals of two crew members, a boatswain and the ship's surgeon. For the funeral of the surgeon, they had to wait two days for the cold to let up, and even then Pastor Jensen had to abbreviate the service, as the cold was so bitter.

After Christmas Pastor Jensen became so weak from poor food and illness that he, like the rest of the crew, could barely survive. By January 23, Pastor Jensen was confined to his bed, and the log records, "Then the priest sat up in his berth and preached a sermon for the men, and that was the last sermon

Drawing from the Munk expedition

he made in this world." Munk later recorded on February 20, 1620, "In the evening died the ship's chaplain, the said Herr Rasmus Jensen, who by this time had long lain sick." Thus ended the career of the first Lutheran pastor in North America. Munk and only two other men survived that brutal winter and made their way back to Denmark.

Believing that he been called to India, Pastor Jensen found himself instead stranded in the harsh winter of the Canadian Arctic. He ministered faithfully to the crew for as long as he was able, leading worship, celebrating the sacraments, and even preaching from his sickbed, until he could no longer do so. He was buried in an unmarked grave on a foreign shore far from home, the first of many brave Lutheran pastors to serve in this New World.

MARK GRANQUIST

Slovak Lutherans: A Tough-minded People

Lutheranism in Europe fared the best in those countries where it was a majority, supported by the government—such as in Scandinavia, the Baltic, and parts of Germany. But the shifting fortunes of religion and politics sometimes stranded Lutheran Christians in areas where they became the religious minority among other Christians. This was a difficult thing for these Lutherans, who often faced neglect and persecution from the majorities around them and who had to struggle to maintain their distinct Lutheran identities. Such was (and is) the case of the Lutherans in the central European country of Slovakia, where centuries of being in the minority have challenged but not destroyed the Lutheran community there.

Movements for reform of the medieval Catholic church took hold in Slovakia in the fifteenth century, 100 years before Martin Luther, through the efforts of reformer Jan Hus and organized groups such as the Hussites and later the Bohemian Brethren. Lutheranism came into Slovakia in the early sixteenth century and was quickly embraced by a good portion of the people, though it was fiercely opposed by the local medieval Catholic hierarchy, with the strong support of the Hungarians rulers of Slovakia. The Roman Catholic attempts to wipe out Protestantism in Slovakia (and elsewhere), called the counter-Reformation, reached their peak in the seventeenth century, when hundreds of Slovak Lutheran pastors were tortured, imprisoned, exiled, and even sold into slavery. The Lutheran churches and population in Slovakia came under tremendous pressure, and many had to go underground to survive. A measure of relief came in the eighteenth century when enlightened rulers came to the throne of the Austro-Hungarian em-

Reformer Jan Hus

pire, but the Lutherans in Slovakia had suffered greatly, and it took a long time for them to recover.

Slovak Lutherans were, however, a stubborn (and even tough) people, and they withstood these centuries of persecution because of their deep commitment to the Lutheran understanding of the Christian faith. The Bible was translated into the local languages in the early sixteenth century, and groups of local cities issued Lutheran confessions of faith, but it was above all their hymns and hymnals that formed the core of their faith, and that held them together during the tough times. Above all was the work of Pastor Jiří Třanovský (1592-1637), who translated the Augsburg Confession into Slovak and produced the hymnal, *Cithara Sanctorum*, which has formed the bedrock of Slovak Lutheranism over the centuries. Two hymns from this hymnal are found in *Evangelical Lutheran Worship*, "Your Heart, O God, Is Grieved" (hymn 602) and "God, my Lord, My Strength" (hymn 795).

Jiří Třanovský

Slovaks began immigrating to the United States around the turn of the twentieth century, settling mainly in mining and industrial areas stretching from Pennsylvania to Wisconsin. The majority of Slovak immigrants were Roman Catholic, but a sizable minority of Slovak Lutherans also came. It is hard to know how many Lutheran Slovaks immigrated, because they were lumped together with oth-

Slovakia today

er ethnic groups, but a rough estimate of Slovak Lutherans in 1960 totaled over 40,000 baptized members in 104 congregations. A substantial number of immigrants came to the United States before and after World War I, and ministry in the Slovak language regularly occurred in these congregations though the 1980s.

Slovak-American Lutherans formed their first organization in 1902, the Slovak Evangelical Lutheran Church (SELC), which affiliated with the Synodical Conference (dominated by the Lutheran Church–Missouri Synod). As a result of internal tensions within the Slovak Lutheran community, about half the Slovaks left the SELC and formed the Slovak Zion Synod in 1918. The Slovak Zion Synod joined with the eastern United Lutheran Church in America in 1920, becoming a non-geographical, ethnic synod within the ULCA, later the LCA, and now in the ELCA. The Slovak Evangelical Lutheran Church changed its name to the Synod of Evangelical Lutheran Churches in 1959, and in 1971 it became a non-geographical district of the Lutheran Church–Missouri Synod, which also remains today. The Slovak Lutheran habit of independence is hard to overcome, and both the SELC and the Slovak Zion Synods maintain a measure of their own autonomy.

Jaroslav Pelikan

One of the most significant Slovak-American Lutherans was Dr. Jaroslav Pelikan, a distinguished theologian and historian.

After World War II, Slovakia was plunged into Communist rule for forty years, its state-atheism again challenging the Slovak Lutherans. Much damage was done to the Lutheran churches in Slovakia during this time, but, since the end of Communism, American Lutherans (Slovaks and others) have worked hard to help rebuild the Slovak Lutheran communities in a newly independent Slovakia. Both the LCMS and the ELCA have sent teachers and assistance to the Slovak Lutherans, and many local congregations have helped in these efforts. Slovak Lutherans are, in many ways, survivors, and 500 years of history and tradition suggest that they will once again rebuild their Lutheran communities.

MARK GRANQUIST

Lutherans in the Caribbean

When winter drags on, many Lutherans in the cold, northern climates begin to think about getting away from the snow and ice, moving somewhere warm. Wouldn't it be nice to settle on a tropical island somewhere, like in the Caribbean, and be done with winter once and for all. So why don't we do this—move to the Caribbean? Well, I know what you are going to say: "I'd love to move to the Caribbean, but then wouldn't it be impossible to find a good Lutheran church?" Well, I have news for you: There *are* Lutherans in the Caribbean! Many of them! (Start packing your boxes.)

There have been Lutherans in some parts of the Caribbean for almost 400 years, and in some other places Lutheranism has been present for equally long periods of time. There are substantial numbers of Lutherans in the Virgin Islands, Puerto Rico, Guyana, and Suriname, with scattered congregations in Antigua, Bermuda, the Bahamas, Cuba, and Haiti. One of the sixty-five synods of the Evangelical Lutheran Church in America is wholy in this area, the Caribbean Synod, which consists of congregations in the Virgin Island

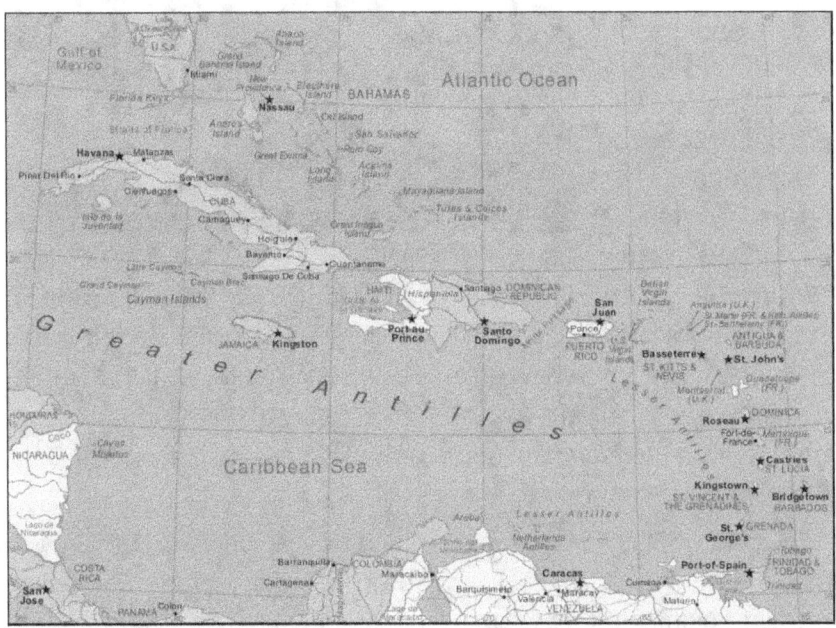

and Puerto Rico. As of 2010, there were more than 27,000 Lutherans around the Caribbean basin.

Historically, Lutheranism came to the Caribbean as the religion of white European, and later, American settlers. But in time some of these churches opened their doors to local inhabitants—Hispanics, African-Americans, and Native Americans—and some of these congregations have become truly indigenous and multicultural ministries. More recently, North Americans moved and settled in some parts of the Caribbean, beginning other congregations for expatriates and vacationers. There is quite a variety of different Caribbean congregations: Some are independent church bodies, while others are related to American Lutheran denominations, such as the Evangelical Lutheran Church in America (ELCA), the Lutheran Church–Missouri Synod (LCMS), and the Wisconsin Evangelical Lutheran Synod (WELS).

The oldest Lutheran congregation in the Caribbean was founded in the Virgin Islands in 1666 by the Danish settlers on the island of St. Croix, the Frederik congregation in Charlotte Amalie. They later founded other congregations on islands of St. Croix, St. John, and St. Thomas in the eighteenth century. Although these congregations were originally intended for Danes, by the 1750s they were doing mission work with the enslaved Africans on the islands. When the Danes sold these islands to the United States in 1917, these congregations affiliated with American Lutheran denominations. There are also several congregations of Virgin Island Lutherans on the mainland of the United States, most notably in New York City.

Frederik Lutheran Church, Charlotte Amalie

Similarly, Dutch Lutherans founded congregations in the area of Guyana and Suriname in the eighteenth century, as the Europeans planted colonies there. Congregations generally consisted of white settlers and their descendants until the middle of the nineteenth century, when they began to reach out to other populations. Guyana is especially racially diverse, and the Lutheran congregations there include African-Americans, Native Americans, East Indians, and some Chinese. Though served by pastors from Europe and America for quite some time, these Lutheran churches eventually became autonomous. These two churches now contain approximately 17,000 members.

Though it has a long history of European colonization, Lutherans did not become established on Puerto Rico until it became a part of the United States in 1898. In that year a young student, Gustav Swenson, moved to Puerto Rico and eventually started a Lutheran congregation there. He was eventually followed by a number of pastors and missionaries from the United States who began to preach in Spanish to the local population. Eventually, by 2005, there were twenty-eight congregations in Puerto Rico, with some 5,000 members, as a part of the Caribbean Synod of the ELCA.

Lutheran congregations exist in some of the other islands of the Caribbean as well. There was a small Lutheran presence in Cuba up to the revolution of 1961, and some scattered congregations may still exist. There is a WELS congregation in Antigua, founded in the 1970s. There is one ELCA congregation in Bermuda, and two Lutheran congregations in the Bahamas, an LCMS congregation in Nassau, and an ELCA congregation in Freeport. There is also a Lutheran presence in Haiti, connected with the Church of the Lutheran Confession in Alsace and Lorraine (France).

Though many of these Caribbean Lutheran congregations were begun by European or Americans, either as settlers or missionaries, most of their members are now predominantly local people—Virgin Islanders, Guyanese and Surinamese, Puerto Ricans, and others. They may be Hispanic, Native American, African-American, or other local populations, worshipping in Spanish, English, French, or other local languages. These congregations enrich the palate of world Lutheranism and help spread the gospel of Christ into every corner of the world.

MARK GRANQUIST

Spener and Pietism

"What would Lutheranism have to show in the cause of world evangelization if it were not for the pietists?"[1] So opines a critic of Pietism who concluded at last that its defects were overshadowed by the renewed interest in missions it stimulated.

"Pietism" is the term applied to a movement beginning in the latter part of the seventeenth century in Germany. Its defenders describe it as a positive response to a drift toward mere formalism among many orthodox Lutherans. Its detractors label it as negative and legalistic and, ultimately, a catalyst for rationalism.

Philip Jacob Spener

Philip Jacob Spener is generally regarded as the "father" of Lutheran Pietism. In 1675, as an attempt to address the spiritual conditions as he viewed them, Spener published his *Pia Desideria*[2] (pious desires) in which he not only offered his analysis of the state of the church but also offered several proposals aimed at renewal of spiritual life.

Lamenting the general lack of Bible knowledge, Spener's first proposal urged a wider diffusion of the Scriptures. He recommended that there be more reading of the Scriptures in public worship. He suggested regular meetings for Bible study and discussion led by pastors. He emphasized the importance of daily Bible reading in the home. Spener was convinced that if only people would expose themselves to the Word of God, spiritual renewal would be the outcome. He said, "The more at home the Word of God is among us, the more we shall bring about faith and its fruits."[3]

---

[1] Newton Flew, *The Idea of Perfection in Christian Theology* (Oxford: Clarendon Press, 1934), 279.

[2] Philip Jacob Spener, *Pia Desideria* (Philadelphia: Fortress Press, 1964).

[3] Ibid., 87.

Reminiscent of Luther's sixteenth century rediscovery of the gospel, Spener called for a renewed appreciation and application of "the priesthood of all believers" (cf. 1 Peter 2:9). Much of the alleged spiritual lethargy was the result of inadequate use of the laity in his estimation. He contended that the common exercise of spiritual gifts was critical to a renewal of spiritual life. The small-group Bible studies (*collegia pietatis*) that emerged as one of the first developments of the Pietist movement provided an opportunity for the use of those gifts.

By the middle of the eighteenth century, Pietism had waned considerably as an identifiable movement. However, its multiplied beneficiaries and adherents continued to make a profound impact in Germany and elsewhere not only on church life but also in society. Pietism emerged ultimately as a vast missionary movement extending the gospel in many parts of the world including colonial America.

Pietism's influence among Lutherans in America is readily observable in several of its church groups. The principal organizer of American Lutheranism, Henry Melchior Muhlenberg, was commissioned to go to America in 1742 by August Hermann Francke, a Pietist leader. The German founders of the first Lutheran congregation in Pennsylvania in the early eighteenth century had brought with them Luther's Bible, his catechism, and a devotional classic used by the Pietists, Johan Arndt's *True Christianity*.

August Hermann Francke

The founder of the Lutheran Church–Missouri Synod, C. F. W. Walther, though eschewing the excesses of later Pietists, had saturated himself with the writings of Spener and Francke as a student in Germany. A deeply pious man, Walther balanced emphasis on doctrinal purity with a living faith.

The ELCA reflects the influence of Pietism among its constituents, particularly those of Scandinavian and Finnish descent. The Norwegian-American descendants in the ELCA as well as in smaller groups such as the Association of Free Lutheran Congregations and the Church of the Lutheran Brethren trace their spiritual moorings in large part to the Pietist revival movements in Scandinavia.

While Pietism as "fathered" by Spener and furthered by a host of others is open for criticism due to aberrations and excesses among its adherents, its positive contributions are many. Central motifs that have ignited spiritual renewal in many lands include:

The centrality of the Bible, inspired, authoritative, and effective in accomplishing God's purpose to save the "lost" and sanctify the "found." To the extent that Pietism has relied on the Word it has made a positive impact.

The necessity of a "living faith." Though the sacraments are efficacious "means of grace," wherein faith is created and nurtured, the baptized need to have a "living faith" which is not mere intellectual assent to the gospel but personal trust in Christ.

The expectation of a godly lifestyle as empowered by the Holy Spirit. True faith is dynamic and invariably results in the emergence of "fruits."

The urgency of missions as incumbent upon the church in every age. From the beginning of Pietism, the missionary enterprise has loomed large as a central purpose of the church.

The best of Pietism has contributed immensely to the progress of the Christian church. May our gracious Lord grant a renewal of the Pietist centralities in our time, all for his glory and the extension of his kingdom.

FRANCIS W. MONSETH

Lutherans in the American South

"Lutherans" and "the American South" are not exactly synonymous in the popular imagination. We think of Baptists in the South and Lutherans in the upper Midwest, but that is to neglect important and long-established American Lutheran communities that stretch from Virginia to Texas. While these southern Lutherans are not large numerically, they have made important contributions to their region and to Lutheranism in America. Historically there were significant Lutheran communities established in the Southeast (Virginia to Georgia) in colonial times, then in Texas in the nineteenth century, and elsewhere in the South (especially in Florida) in the twentieth century. The South is also home to important communities of African-American and Hispanic Lutherans.

Many of the German Lutheran immigrants to colonial America settled in Pennsylvania, but in search of free land some Lutherans began to move down into the western regions of Virginia (the Shenandoah Valley) as early as the 1710s, from there moving down into western North Carolina. Beginning in the 1730s other German immigrants came into South Carolina and settled in the upland areas around Columbia. At the same time, a group of Lutheran Salzburg refugees settled in Georgia. Initially there were severe shortages of resources and pastors, but many of these Lutherans managed to form congregations. Though some of them suffered during the Revolutionary War, these congregations managed to grow. Eventually in the nineteenth century Lutherans established synods in Virginia and North and South Carolina. Doctrinal differences led to the formation of the Tennessee Synod on this same territory.

Although some of the first southern Lutherans were opposed to slavery, some of them eventually owned slaves, or at least came to support this "institution" as necessary for their society. Before the Civil War some Lutheran congregations consisted of both whites and African-Americans (but the latter were not equal). During the war southern Lutherans formed their synods into a regional organization, the General Synod South. This was continued after the war and later expanded as the United Synod of the South. Southern Lutherans remained apart from their colleagues in the North until 1918, when they joined with other Lutheran in the colonial (Muhlenberg) tradition to form the United Lutheran Church in America. After the war many African-American Lutherans were excluded from white congregations. They were encouraged to form separate Lutheran congregations, but these struggled from a lack of resources.

The great migration of European Lutherans to the United States from 1840 to 1920 was mainly focused on the American Midwest, and few Lutheran immigrants settled directly in the South. There was one exception, however, and that was the state of Texas. Early German communities were formed in central Texas beginning in the 1840s, and there were also settlements of Swedes and Norwegians. Germans formed the Texas Synod in 1851, while the Scandinavian congregations affiliated with their own national denominations. Though primarily a midwestern group, the Lutheran Church–Missouri Synod extended its work into Texas and the southeastern states, forming congregations there. The Missouri Synod also began work with African-Americans (including Lutherans) in the South and established congregations and educational institutions there.

In the nineteenth century, American Lutherans founded important educational and social service institutions in the South. The Lutheran Theological Southern Seminary was begun in 1830, as well as colleges in the southeastern states and Texas. The Missouri Synod established schools for African-Americans in North Carolina, New Orleans, and Alabama; the latter, Concordia College Alabama, in Selma, remains as one of the historically black colleges.

After about 1880, some Americans (tired of the northern weather or attracted by opportunities) began to migrate to the South, especially to Florida. They formed Lutheran congregations, usually affiliated with northern denominations. These initial communities were augmented by the great wave of internal migration to the South after World War II. Scores of new Lutheran mission congregations were formed in the South in the 1950s and 1960s, swelling the numbers of Lutherans there (especially in Florida and Texas). With the mergers of the 1960s, and the formation of the Evangelical Lutheran Church in America in 1988, many southern Lutherans were joined together. A significant number of others are affiliated with the Lutheran Church–Missouri Synod.

Even with this growth, Lutherans remain only a small part of the whole of the South, where the Baptist, Methodist, and Pentecostal churches predominate. The historic, "colonial" Lutherans in the southeastern states have long held to their communities, forming what might be called a separate tradition (or even "ethnicity") among their neighbors, where it is at times difficult to maintain a Lutheran confessional identity in the midst of so many others. Newer Lutherans in the South have sometimes been tempted to see their congregations as "outposts" of northern or "ethnic" Lutheranism, but have slowly become a part of their region. These southern Lutherans stand as an important and distinctive part of Lutheranism in America.

MARK GRANQUIST

Schwartz Reaches Out to India

During the half-century Christian Friedrich Schwartz labored in South India, Lutherans there were occupied with forming congregations, a series of wars, and figuring out how to be Christians among a Hindu population, soon to be under British rule. In the same years Lutherans in North America were occupied with forming congregations, the American Revolution, and figuring out how to be citizens of a nation newly free of British rule. Schwartz was one of a series of pastoral leaders trained at the Halle Institutions, a center of German Pietism, who were sent to serve in both places. Along with theological studies, these men absorbed the Halle model of Christian mission that cultivated a warm spirituality and gave service to the whole person through schools as well as preaching.

Christian Friedrich Schwartz

Inspired by stories of earlier missionaries, Henry Melchior Muhlenberg, the so-called patriarch of American Lutheranism, contemplated a call to serve in India. However, he was sent instead to Pennsylvania in the early 1740s. Once settled, he took up his work and gathered scattered Lutherans into an organized church body. Half a generation younger, Christian Friedrich Schwartz (1726-98) studied at Halle, was ordained in Copenhagen, and preached in London before he reached the Danish colony of Tranquebar in 1750. There he joined the lineage of missionaries begun in 1706 by fellow Germans Bartholomäus Ziegenbalg and Henry Plutschau under the sponsorship of the Danish king.

Throughout his ministry in South India, Schwartz emulated his predecessors and went beyond them. He equipped local leaders for the growing Tamil evangelical churches, established schools, ministered to soldiers, supervised relief for victims of war, and served as a diplomatic emissary between the British and local rulers. After a decade stationed in Tranquebar, Schwartz shifted his work first to the English garrison in Trichinoply (1762-72) and then to the princely state of Tanjore (1772-98). After 1767 Schwartz was supported by the English Society for Promoting Christian Knowledge.

Like Muhlenberg in Pennsylvania, Schwartz was met by a growing Christian community. When he arrived in India, he joined three ordained Tamil preachers (Aaron, Diago, and Rajanayagam), a handful of other European missionaries, dozens of Tamil teacher pastors, and nearly 17,000 Christian believers. His work took him outside church circles into contact with British merchants and administrators as well as Indian rulers. In order to carry out his work, he supplemented his previous study of Tamil and English with study of other Indian languages, Persian, and Portuguese. His "directness, truth speaking, and piety" (IVP, p. 81) earned him the trust and admiration of Indians and Europeans, of Christians, Hindus, and Muslims.

The mission program developed in Halle regarded literacy and access to the Bible in one's native language as an essential foundation of Christian life. Beginning with Ziegenbalg, Schwartz' predecessors had launched translation and publication projects that produced Tamil editions of the Bible and other Christian materials. Early converts composed Christian songs and literature in indigenous forms. Schwartz helped to build up the Tamil church by preparing and supporting Indian leaders and by contributing to construction of new facilities for worship and education.

Schwartz continued the practice of sending pairs of Indian Christians into villages to evangelize and to educate believers. Often he accompanied these workers on their rounds. Every congregation was to have a school, a catechist, and a *panchayat*, or governing council. These workers gathered at the beginning and end of the day for prayers with Schwartz as well as for monthly training sessions. On several occasions he was paid by secular authorities for services such as supervising food relief in time of famine or tending to the spiritual needs of English soldiers. These funds he designated for building schools or churches, rather than for his own use.

By establishing schools, preparing Indian catechists and pastors, and preaching the gospel Schwartz did what was expected of a

Halle-trained missionary in South Asia or North America. What distinguished Schwartz was his abiding concern for the welfare of the people beyond the realm of church. Perhaps this is illustrated most vividly in his diplomatic mission to Hyder Ali, ruler of Mysore, on behalf of the British East India Company. Unfortunately, although Schwartz received a hospitable reception, relations remained tense and Hyder Ali invaded Tanjore in 1781. Less dramatically, Schwartz served as chaplain to soldiers, both English and Indian, wounded in ongoing battles between English and French forces and their Indian allies.

Along with a financial endowment to support Christian mission, Schwartz's legacy to South India was a cadre of leaders who regarded him as their father as well as their teacher. Among these was young Serfoji, who would become the Maharaj of Tanjore, and Christian poet and hymn writer, Vandanayaka Sastri. Under Schwartz's direction, the boys were tutored in a wide array of topics worthy of the Halle model including Bible, mathematics, leadership, and emerging European models of science. Serfoji erected a marble monument to Schwartz's memory, but the schools the Maharaj sponsored for his subjects and his life-long friendship with Vandanayaka Sastri were a living memorial to the missionary's godly efforts to secure peace and the well-being of the people of South India, Christian and non-Christian alike.

Engraving of Schwartz with Prince Serfoji II

L. DEANE LAGERQUIST

From Salzburg to Georgia

Being Lutheran was not easy in the region around Salzburg in Austria in the early eighteenth century. By the end of 1731, it was not even permissible. On November 11 of that year, the Archbishop of Salzburg issued a decree giving Lutherans in the territory two choices—convert to Catholicism or leave.

The order kept the arrangement made following the religious wars stemming from the Protestant Reformation. Under the treaty that ended the Thirty Years' War in 1648, the ruler of a territory determined which religion—Catholic, Lutheran, or Calvinist—would be permitted in that territory. For practical reasons, rulers did not always enforce the decree. But by the end of the 1720s, Salzburg's Catholic archbishop, who also held the political authority for his territory, decided the time had come.

Within a year, about 20,000 Lutherans left. Most journeyed north to settle in Prussia in eastern Germany or in the Netherlands. But for forty-one religious exiles, another destination awaited. England needed settlers for a new colony. The colony's organizers, aware through their German connections that these Salzburgers needed a home, offered to settle the emigrants in the land soon to called Georgia, named after England's King George II.

Johann Martin Boltzius

By the end of 1733, the rag-tag group of exiles had made their way to Rotterdam. Joining them there were the two pastors appointed to lead them across the Atlantic and into their new life in America. Johann Martin Boltzius and Israel Christian Gronau had been educated in Halle, Germany, the center of German Pietism, a brand of Lutheranism that stressed the practice of Christian faith in a life of inward spiritual experience and outward service. From Rotterdam the group sailed to England, and from England to America, arriving in Savannah on March 12, 1734.

A house built and occupied by the Salzburger settlers in Georgia

James Oglethorpe, the governor of the colony, assigned to the Salzburgers a plot of land along the Savannah River, about four hours' boat ride, or twenty-five miles, from the town of Savannah. The exiles named their settlement Ebenezer, "Thus far has God helped us" (1 Samuel 7:12).

When the land proved unsuitable, the fledging community relocated a few miles to New Ebenezer. Here, the people and their pastors resumed building their town and their lives. In time, houses replaced huts and the community expanded beyond the confines of their small town to larger farms in the surrounding area. Their numbers also grew as children were born as well as by the addition of more transports of emigrants who made the voyage across the Atlantic. Not all of these newcomers were Salzburgers, but rather natives of the German territory of Swabia. By the early 1740s, the population of Ebenezer reached close to 250 adults and children.

But adjusting to the new land provided major challenges. Illness, especially in the form of malaria, became a constant companion. Pastor Boltzius himself battled malaria off and on for the better part of twenty years. Tragedy struck when the Israel Gronau, the junior of the two pastors, died in 1745. The community also struggled to develop a healthy economic life through agriculture, milling, silk-making, and lumber.

Circumstances in Georgia brought their share of surprises—Boltzius reports his first encounter with a new root called a "potato"—and also disappointments. Missionary work among the Indians did not yield the results Boltzius had hoped and, despite the pastor's best efforts, slavery eventually made its way into the colony and into Ebenezer.

From Ebenezer, Boltzius gained a vantage point for observing the religious life of the American colonies. He became acquainted with John Wesley while the future Methodist leader served as an Anglican priest in Savannah. And he followed the situations of Lutherans in neighboring South Carolina and as far away as Pennsylvania. Henry Melchior Muhlenberg, the future leader of Lutheranism there, made Ebenezer his first stop, meeting with Boltzius before undertaking his own ministry to the north.

By the time Boltzius died in 1765, the town of Ebenezer already was in decline, in large measure because of the success of the surrounding farms where the colonists settled. But the legacy remains. Jerusalem Lutheran Church continues as an active Lutheran congregation on the site of the settlement. The sanctuary, envisioned by Boltzius but constructed a few years after his death, is the second to occupy the site. Visitors who look closely at the bricks of the building can still see the imprints of fingers that made them. A vibrant retreat and conference center also welcomes thousands of visitors every year at the location once planned as the settlers' permanent home.

Jerusalem Lutheran Church, Ebenezer, Georgia

From forty-one originals exiles and their two pastors, across an ocean and across more than two and a half centuries, the legacy continues in the descendents of those original settlers who left Europe and made Ebenezer their home.

RUSSELL C. KLECKLEY

Lutherans and Native Americans

Most European Lutherans immigrating to North America were in search of good farmland on which they could settle—this was the dream of America. Unfortunately their dreams were in reality nightmares to the native people who were already living on those lands when the Europeans arrived. The Native Americans were systematically pushed off their lands, ever westward, until they were forced onto reservations. Disease, exploitation, the destruction of their cultures and ways of life were devastating to the original inhabitants of this country, and the effects of this still plague their communities today. Religious groups sometimes sought to assist the Native Americans, but their efforts were sporadic at best, and all too often these groups were complicit with policies that made life even worse for native peoples.

During the colonial period, there were occasional contacts between the newly-arrived Lutherans and the Native Americans. In the New Sweden colony, Pastor John Campanius (pastor on the Delaware from 1643 to 1648) had good relations with the local Lenape tribe and even learned their language so as to translate Luther's *Small Catechism* into Algonquin. Published in Sweden in 1696 and sent back to America, there is no record of it ever being used. Colonial Lutheran pastors on the frontiers in New York and Georgia had occasional contacts with Native Americans and may even have baptized a few. European church leaders urged further missionary outreach, but a severe lack of resources made this impossible. Pastor John C. Hartwick in upstate New York left his property to fund a school for Native Americans, but this project never reached its intended audience.

New Sweden

As American pushed westward after the Revolutionary War, they pushed the native people out of their way, aided by government policies. The Native Americans were an inconvenient and threatening "other," a "problem" to be addressed. At this time Lutheranism in America was still a mission field of its own, without enough resources to manage its own population. But Lutherans did attempt some mission with native peoples. The most interesting of these was by German Lutheran settlers in Michigan, led by Lutheran pastors sent from Germany by Wilhelm Löhe. Starting in 1845 these pastors worked among both the immigrants and the local native peoples, establishing congregations and schools for both populations. For a brief time this outreach produced results, until the native people were pushed off their lands and farther westward. Some of these Löhe missionaries also moved west and founded the Iowa Synod. In the 1850s and 1860s this group sent missionaries out to the native people in Wyoming and Montana, without permanent results.

Immigrant Lutheran groups began occasional mission work among Native Americans in the latter part of the nineteenth century. Swedish Lutherans from the Augustana Synod surveyed parts of the west for possible mission opportunities during the 1870s, but nothing came of this. In 1884 the Norwegian Synod initiated efforts in Wisconsin among the Winnebago tribe; this Bethany Mission lasted until 1955. Danish American Lutherans took over a mission among the Cherokee in Oaks, Oklahoma, in 1892, and a congregation there is still in existence. In 1893 the Wisconsin Evangelical Lutheran Synod sent missionaries to begin work with Apaches in Arizona, and that

The Bethany Indian Mission and School, Wittenberg, Wisconsin

mission in still in existence. In 1894, Norwegian Synod Pastor T. L. Brevig was sent to Alaska; his initial outreach with Sami (Lapp) reindeer herders sent to Alaska did not work, but Brevig developed an outreach to native tribes around the remote village of Teller. This outreach resulted in several permanent native congregations. In 1899 the Missouri Synod initiated an effort among the Stockbridge tribe in Wisconsin.

In the twentieth century, some of these outreach programs were transformed into local congregations or were phased out. New efforts at mission with native communities were begun. In 1928 agencies of the United Lutheran Church in American took on work on the Rocky Boy's Reservation in north central Montana. In 1970 Pastor Les Stahlke began LAMP (now Lutheran Association of Missionaries and Pilots) to provide ministry to remote First Nations communities in the Canadian Arctic by means of missionary pilots and other volunteers. An associated group in the United States runs its programs through the Lutheran Indian Ministries, recognized by the Lutheran Church–Missouri Synod. Currently the Evangelical Lutheran Church in America has an American Indian/Native Alaskan membership of about 4,900 in thirty native congregations and other ministries. The Wisconsin Evangelical Lutheran Synod maintains its Apache schools and congregations in Arizona.

Lutherans have also done advocacy work alongside native communities, most noticeably the controversial role that the Rev. Paul Boe and the American Lutheran Church played in assisting the formation of the American Indian Movement (AIM). Boe was later drawn into the events of the Wounded Knee uprising in 1973 and came under investigation and prosecution by the U.S. federal government, though he was eventually cleared of charges.

MARK GRANQUIST

Henry Melchior Muhlenberg: A Leader of American Lutherans

One of the most important and influential American Lutherans that ever lived was born 300 year ago in Hanover, Germany. Henry Melchior Muhlenberg (1711-1787) came from a middle-class family, but through his efforts (and with some aid) became a pastor. In 1741 he was commissioned as a missionary; though his first desire was to go to India, he was sent instead to several Lutheran congregations near Philadelphia, where he arrived in November 1742.

Muhlenberg found upon his arrival in North America a growing Lutheran population but one that was weakly organized, poorly led, and riddled by disputes. For the next forty-five years, though his call was primarily to serve the Philadelphia congregations, in reality he became the acknowledged leader of most Lutherans in North America. Muhlenberg organized the first synodical organization of American Lutherans in 1748—the Ministerium of Pennsylvania—and provided it with a constitution, liturgy, and hymnbook.

Henry Melchior Muhlenberg

His direct influence covered Lutheran congregations from New York to Virginia and occasionally as far south as Georgia. He traveled constantly, founding new congregations, maintaining established ones, and frequently arbitrating disputes among and within them. He also served as an influential leader for German-Americans in colonial America and became adept in defending Lutheran interests in the tempestuous world of colonial politics, especially during the traumas of the Revolutionary War.

Seal of the Ministerium of Pennsilvania

When Muhlenberg arrived in North America he had little direct support or money, and initially had to deal with direct opposition from elements of his congregation. The transition to the North American context was very difficult for the Lutherans who encountered a strange new world of voluntary pluralism and democracy, no state support, and the religious domination of English-speaking Reformed Protestants. Muhlenberg worked especially closely with other German-American Protestants—Reformed, Moravian, and others—but also worked with the "English" (as in, English-speaking) churches around him. Though firmly Lutheran, he was open to new groups and peoples. He knew and advocated for Native Americans and called for the evangelization of enslaved African-Americans. He also provided occasional pastoral services to African-Americans in Philadelphia at no charge. He was acquainted with many of the colonial religious and political leaders, such as colonial evangelist George Whitefield and Benjamin Franklin.

As Muhlenberg struggled to establish and define his vision of Lutheranism in the American colonies, he had direct competition from three other groups. In New York and New Jersey, the Lutheran leader was William Berkenmeyer, a German pastor sent to America by the Lutheran church in Hamburg.

Muhlenberg's home in Trappe, Pennsylvania

In Pennsylvania and the middle colonies, there was an established group of German Moravians under the guidance of Count Nicolas Ludwig von Zinzendorf. And because of its religious toleration, Pennsylvania was the home to numerous different groups of German Anabaptists and Radical Pietists, including Mennonites, Amish, Dunkers, and Brethren.

Berkenmeyer was too rigid in his approach and unable to adapt to the new American context, so he was drawn into numerous battles among local pastors and congregations. Muhlenberg was unwillingly dragged into a number of these conflicts but often was able to bring about resolution where Berkenmeyer could not. Increasingly, Muhlenberg's influence grew among the New York and New Jersey congregations. When Berkenmeyer died in 1751, Muhlenberg faced little competition for control from other local Lutheran pastors.

Nicolas Ludwig von Zinzendorf

In the 1740s Zinzendorf made two trips to North America to promote his union plans, and when he failed to push them through, he turned to meddling in local Lutheran congregations, seeking to place Moravian preachers in Lutheran parishes. This was a direct and immediate threat to Muhlenberg when he arrived in 1742, and he worked hard to counter the Moravian influence among the Lutherans, which faded after 1748. In a similar vein but much less organized, the German Radical Pietist and Anabaptist groups also sought to gather immigrant Germans into their congregations, and away from Muhlenberg's Lutheran congregations.

In all of this, Muhlenberg sought a center position. The Lutheranism that Muhlenberg established in North America was essentially a "churchly" Pietism, a moderate form of Pietism that sought to work within the confessional boundaries of Lutheranism, warmed by a healthy dose of Pietist spirituality. This movement took a broad view of the Christian community and essentially held to a "folk church" understanding of the Christian community. While stressing the Lutheran centrality of justification, it also maintained a parallel sense of sanctification, with an emphasis on a life lived in response to grace. In his congregations he stressed living a life of personal moral integrity, the duty of all Christians to share the gospel, and the Bible as the central living narrative that informs the Christian life. It was this sense of the church and Christian life, and the ways in which they were formed in an American context, that was Muhlenberg's lasting contribution to American Lutheranism.

MARK GRANQUIST

Colonial Lutheran Pastoral Care

The life of a Lutheran pastor in colonial America was difficult. Without much of anything in the way of material support, pastors struggled just to survive, let alone care for their poor and scattered flocks. They had be prepared to meet many different kinds of situations never envisioned in their European ministerial training. Yet a number of them gave devoted and heroic service in the new American colonies, proclaiming the gospel and guiding their people as best they could. The following entries from the notebooks of colonial Lutheran leader Henry Melchior Muhlenberg illustrate their lives and ministries. These selections are culled from just one month, November 1763 (note: these entries are much condensed).

Henry Melchior Muhlenberg

> November 1: In the forenoon I had all sorts of running in and out and troublesome interruptions. Visit from the late Pastor Steiner's widow, who had many laments to make.

> November 5: Saturday. Visit from Josua Pawling, of Providence, who said I must again take over the Providence church and congregation, otherwise everything would go to ruin.

> November 6: I went to church with Mr. Brycelius, baptized three children, and preached to a crowded auditorium. As soon as church was over I was taken to Germantown to bury Mr. Jacob Gänsle. About five-thirty in the evening I drove away and arrived home in the dark near eight o'clock.

> November 9: I felt unwell, but I had to carry out my promise to go to Mr. [George] Whitefield. He received us very cordially. I received a courteous letter inviting me to visit Chief Judge Coleman and furnish a testimonial to the deceased

wife of a certain Lutheran man. I also visited the silversmith, Mr. Carben; had a refreshing visit with the family.

November 13: Sunday. Early in the morning Mr. Jacob Graef took me to Germantown. At eleven o'clock we went to church [and] I preached on the Gospel. My companion drove me back to Philadelphia, but we had to drive very fast to be able to hold the [funeral] service at the right time. After the service I baptized Gr---'s sick child. In the evening I married a couple, then went to the home of Mr. Graef where I found a fine group of awakened members of the congregation [and] had an edifying and inspirational conversation with them from seven to nine o'clock.

November 16: Learned that the church council had rejected the petitions I had submitted to them. This bewildering and miserable affair is hastening my death and is almost rendering me unfit for my office.

November 17: Today we had the first deep snow and unhealthy, wet weather. Had a visit. . . . The rest of the time I meditated and wrote. Otherwise I was distressed and depressed over the intricate dispute in this poor congregation . . . my health is suffering from it.

November 21: Visit from the poor widow of a Reformed preacher. She was in great straits and besought me to be surety for her, but I was unable to do so. Today I borrowed £50 currency at interest in order to meet my needs. At home I had many visitors, among them a young blacksmith who some year

A monument to Muhlenberg, on Germantown Avenue in Philadelphia, shows him preaching to his congregation

ago had married an old widow [who now] refused to live with him.

The said blacksmith asked me whether he might now marry someone else. Reply: No.

November 22: More and more murders and burnings are occurring on the frontiers, and almost daily there are robberies in and around the city. The city itself is swarming with unruly mobs. I visited a godly family which had retained much of last Sunday's sermon and gained consolation from it.

November 25: Last night I was unable to sleep because of worry and concern of soul about the coming church council meeting and the fact that old quarrels are to be brought up again. I took refuge in quiet prayer to Almighty God [after a long meeting it was noted] .The entire church council and the complainants have settled all points of controversy and made peace. Henceforth there shall be no further discussion or mention of the old controversy.

November 29: Tuesday. Early in the morning I journeyed to Germantown. At home I heard that immediately after my departure on Saturday several dissatisfied persons had come into my house and blustered against me and the church council. At 1 pm I married Daniel Sorg and Margretha Heidel. In the evening we had a heavy rainstorm. Refreshing visit from Mr. Kressler.

November 30: A visit from [Swedish pastor] Wangel, with whom I conferred on various matters and strengthened myself. In the evening I read the *History of the Martyrs* to my family for edification.

(from *The Journals of Henry Melchior Muhlenberg*, vol. 1, pp. 700-716)

MARK GRANQUIST

Father Heyer: On the Move for the Lord

There are those Christians who simply cannot see a need somewhere, without trying to do something about it. When there people on the margins who need to hear the Good News of Jesus Christ proclaimed to them, these Christians jump in without any thought of themselves—they just know that there is a need and someone who needs the proclamation of God's love. An outstanding example of such a Christian was Pastor John Christian Frederick Heyer (1793-1873), commonly known as Father Heyer. He was always on the move, bringing God's Word to those in need, literally around the world.

Heyer migrated from Germany to the United States at the age of fourteen, in 1807. Inspired by Pastor J. H. C. Helmuth, Heyer began his theological studies with him, later returning to Europe to continue his work at the University of Goettingen. Returning to America in 1816, he was immediately assigned to several congregations and was ordained in 1819. For the next decade Heyer served several congregations in western Pennsylvania and by all accounts was a very effective pastor, even learning enough English to becomes a proficient preacher in that new language—quite an accomplishment. Yet Heyer knew that there were Lutherans all over the nation who had neither congregations nor pastors, and this was not acceptable to him.

John Christian Frederick Heyer

At this time, early in the nineteenth century, there was an immense shortage of Lutheran pastors in America, made worse by the fact that Americans of all varieties were headed out to the new lands of the West, where there were no towns and no churches. On the frontier scattered knots of Lutherans gathered for devotions as best they could, but it might be months or years between visits from Lutheran pastors. Many joined the local Methodist or Baptist congregations instead. During his early pastoral career Heyer had attempted to meet these needs locally, but he knew that something more was required. Although by all accounts he was a highly successful parish pastor and could have had his choice of comfortable and established Lutheran congregations, he was drawn to the frontier and to the needs of the people there. From 1830 to 1837 Heyer was commissioned as a wandering Lutheran home missionary, forgoing the comforts of home for the rigors of the frontier. He traveled thousands of miles through wilderness and prairies, meeting constantly with groups of Lutherans and founding dozens of congregations in Ohio, Indiana, Kentucky, and Illinois. In a typical report to Lutherans "back East" he wrote, "In April I have traveled 600 miles, preached fourteen or fifteen times, baptized thirteen, and administered the Lord's Supper to more than a hundred communicants."[1] After years of service, Heyer returned to Pittsburgh, where he founded three Lutheran congregations in a three-year period. No one would have blamed him if he had then settled in for a comfortable parish—he had earned it. But not so Father Heyer.

Father Heyer

Even though they had a difficult time simply meeting the religious needs in their own country, American Lutherans were also aware of the need for missionaries around the world; among them was Father Heyer. In 1840 an American Lutheran organization was looking to send a missionary to India; they chose Heyer, who accepted the call. After studying medicine and Sanskrit, he headed to India, working on the eastern side of the country at Guntur and later Rajahmundry where German Lutheran missionaries had started work. He worked there from 1842 to 1857, and despite a lack of support he developed a thriving mission church.

In 1857 he was sixty-four years old and could have eased into retirement, but that was not his way. Another frontier beckoned. This time it was the upper Mississippi valley, where he spent another decade traveling to distant settlements, ministering to scattered peo-

---

1 E. Theodore Bachman, *They Called Him Father: The Life Story of John Christian Frederick Heyer* (Philadelphia: Muhlenberg Press, 1942), 90.

ple, and forming new congregations, especially in Minnesota. In a number of different trips to the region, he gathered together dozens of congregations and helped form the Minnesota Synod. In 1868, at age seventy-five, Heyer attempted again to retire. However, acute problems at Rajahmundry, India, had developed, so he went in 1870 and was able to revitalize the mission there. Returning to the United States, he spent his last years as a chaplain at the Lutheran seminary in Philadelphia. His mission work finally ended upon his death, November 7, 1873, at age eighty.

Had Heyer accomplished just one of these jobs—pastor, home missionary, or foreign missionary—he would have been well remembered. But it was his constant attention to the religious needs of those without the consolation of the gospel that made him truly remarkable. He gave his life and his whole energy to doing God's work in this world.

MARK GRANQUIST

"Praise the Lord:" Lutherans and American Revivalism

When thinking about American revivalism, many images come to mind: Tent-meeting revival services on the edge of small southern towns, with sawdust, pounding gospel music, and hell-fire preaching. Perhaps a Billy Graham crusades in a big city auditorium, with the music of George Beverly Shea and the final altar call invitation to the music of "Just As I Am." Or perhaps Dwight Lyman Moody or Billy Sunday. But my guess is that you would never associate revivalism with American Lutherans. Guess what? Some American Lutherans did practice revivalism, and many congregations still do use elements of the evangelistic approaches honed in the fire of American revivalism. American religion was fundamentally shaped by revivalism.

Revivalism as we now know it developed after the American Revolution, during the period from 1790 to 1810 called the "Second Great Awakening." Organized religion was very weak in colonial America, and when, after the war, Americans started pouring into the frontier areas west of the Allegany mountains, Christian churches faced an almost impossible task in "churching" this new territory. Too few in numbers to reach the settlers in any traditional ways, pioneering

A revival meeting

preachers had to develop new techniques to match the new situation. Methodist circuit riders and Baptist lay preachers went wherever they needed to reach the settlers. Other preachers decided to gather settlers from far and wide in "camp meetings," where preaching and socializing went hand-in-hand. Unable to reach most settlers consistently for long periods of time, preachers pioneered new ways of influencing their audiences with an emotional, immediate offer of salvation—one that hit home to thousands of people at a time.

News of these great and wonderful revivals of religion from the American frontier filtered back to settled congregations and preachers along the eastern seaboard, and excited spontaneous revivals there too. A New York lawyer-turned-preacher, Charles Grandison Finney, reasoned that these spontaneous revivals could in fact be turned into planned revivals orchestrated to reach masses of unchurched people in the new American republic. Using Finney's techniques, nineteenth-century American preachers brought millions of new converts into formal affiliations with Protestant congregations. Moody, Sunday, and Graham took the basic elements of American revivalism and adjusted them for urban audiences and modern listeners.

Charles Grandison Finney

With all the religious excitement going on around them, American Lutherans could not help but be swept up in revivalism. In the period before the Civil War (1800-1860), many American Lutheran pastors cooperated with other Protestant leaders to organize area-wide revivals, and they also held Lutheran revival services in their congregations and among their institutions. These pastors saw the hand of God at work in the revival, bringing about a new wave of reform in American Lutheranism. One account of a four-day revival among Lutherans in South Carolina in 1831 approvingly reported that "hundreds were bathed in tears, a solemnity pervaded the whole assembly, more than one hundred individuals accepted the invitation given to those who desired to be personally conversed with on the subject of their soul's salvation." Hundreds of such accounts were regularly published in some of the Lutheran newspapers of the time.

This is not to say that revivalism was universally or uncritically accepted among American Lutherans. There were some wilder elements of American revivalism, including emotional outbursts and intense pressure that most Lutherans rejected. In 1841 one Ohio Lutheran synod passed a resolution on revivals that stated that they "recommend opposition to all disorder and ultraism [while] we earnestly encourage our Churches to promote genuine revivals by faithful preaching of the word, by prayer, and by other means in accord with the holy religion of our Redeemer." But more moderated forms of revivalism gained widespread acceptance within Lutheran congregations, though most agreed that conversions gained in such situations needed to be followed up with further Christian education.

Other Lutherans, however, totally rejected American revivalism as being un-Lutheran and un-Christian. One angry writer in 1838 chastised a Lutheran newspaper editor for his eager support of revivals, saying, "You and the other Revival Boys are advocating this Rail-Road Christianity according to which they become sinlessly perfect in an hour (so that) our people might not desert to the Methodists." Newly arrived Lutheran immigrant pastors, along with other conservative Lutheran preachers, spoke out regularly against revivalism and for traditional Lutheran worship. Nothing new about the contemporary American Lutheran "worship wars."

Revivalism remained important in American religion, and one can trace elements of it in many areas still today. For example, the revival tradition of "camp meetings" eventually evolved into the Bible camps that we know today. Gospel songs and direct preaching of the gospel for repentance and the amendment of life remain important in many congregations. If the historic revivals have become a bit of a caricature, many of their effects and techniques are still an important part of American Protestantism, even American Lutheranism.

MARK GRANQUIST

20
Löhe: The Man Who Wouldn't Take No for an Answer

Try to imagine this. You arrive at Christmas Eve worship at your local Lutheran congregation and hear the gospel story about shepherds arriving at the manger. But on the basis of that text, the pastor preaches about the care and feeding of animals!

That was the sort of thing that occurred during what church historians call the Age of Rationalism. That was the kind of world, in 1808, into which Johann Konrad Wilhelm Löhe was born. An outgrowth of the secular Age of Enlightenment in Europe, rationalism seemed to take the churches captive. The idea was, if you can't prove it, don't believe it. Miracles were out of favor, as well as any thought of the supernatural. In that climate, it's not difficult to understand why young Pastor Löhe came to embrace and become a cheerleader for the Lutheran Confessions. "Confessionalists" had no use for rationalism.

Johann Konrad Wilhelm Löhe

The spirit of the times in the German Lutheran Church of the 1800s was such that Löhe's superiors didn't like the young upstart pastor/theologian very much. They thought he was hopelessly old-fashioned and decided to deny him a position in a prestigious congregation anywhere in his native Bavaria. (Such coveted parishes would have included historic St. Sebald Church or equally desirable St. Lorenz, both in old city Nuremburg.)

Instead Löhe was consigned to a hamlet (a mudhole, some would have said) with a nearly unspellable and almost unpronounceable name—Neuendettelsau. The Lutheran congregation there was marginal, and its members largely uneducated.

Clearly his superiors believed they had successfully taught Löhe a lesson by sending him to the Bavarian boondocks. What they were

The Deaconness Motherhouse in Neuendettelsau

really saying to him was, "Wilhelm, you're not pastoral material. You don't belong on the clergy roster."

But Löhe wouldn't take no for an answer.

During his long ministry in Neuendettelsau, this brilliant, thoughtful, passionate, frequently stubborn churchman worked a miracle—in an age when miracles were out of fashion! Empowered by the Holy Spirit, he grew the small parish church into a thriving ministry center. But that wasn't all. Under Löhe's leadership, the community and the congregation founded agencies of mercy—a Lutheran deaconess motherhouse, an orphanage, an improved local school system, and a Lutheran Society for Inner Mission.

And Löhe's vision extended far beyond Neuendettelsau. He had a heart for people in lands where Christianity had not yet reached. Under his direction a Lutheran mission field was planted in faraway New Guinea, an island north of Australia.

Löhe became aware that German Lutherans were immigrating to the American frontier. He recruited and sent to North America an impressive number of clergy—all committed to the confessions of the Lutheran church. He also identified revenue sources to provide salaries for the overseas clergy and to help fund new schools on the other side of the Atlantic.

Named for the Franconian region of Bavaria, a series of Löhe-sponsored settlements sprang up in Michigan, in the region east of present-day Saginaw. They had names like Frankentrost, Frankenlust, and Frankenmuth. The latter community is the home of St. Lorenz Lutheran Church, one of the five founding congregations of the Lutheran Church–Missouri Synod (LCMS).

In Saginaw, some of the "Löhe men" founded a school to train pastors and teachers. This fledgling institution, begun in 1852, would, after several starts and stumbles, give rise to what eventually became Wartburg College in Waverly, Iowa, and Wartburg Theological Seminary in Dubuque. But there was soon a falling out between the school's founders and pastors loyal to the LCMS. It quickly became clear there was to be no reconciliation, so the Löhe contingent packed up their school—teachers, books, and students—and moved to Iowa.

With this stormy and uncertain beginning, the Joint Synod of Iowa and Other States came into being. Until his death in 1872, Löhe, who never came to North America, sent pastors and money to the German Lutherans in Iowa.

The Iowa Synod grew into a sizeable church body. A pair of gifted theologians, Sigmund and Gottfried Fritschel, taught for generations at its seminary in Dubuque. During their tenure theological conflict with the Missouri Synod became intense. At stake was the interpretation of Scripture. The Iowa Synod theologians made a lasting contribution to American Lutheran church life with their contention that Holy Scripture does not definitively settle everything where faith and life are concerned. There are, they maintained, "open questions."

In 1930 the Iowa Synod merged with the Ohio and Buffalo Synods to create the American Lutheran Church (a German body). Thirty years later, this denomination combined with Norwegian and Danish Lutherans to become the (new) American Lutheran Church. Twenty-eight years later, they became part of the Evangelical Lutheran Church in America.

MICHAEL L. SHERER

C. F. W. Walther: Founder of the Lutheran Church–Missouri Synod

Historians sometime debate which is more important: the great and powerful mass movements rolling like tidal waves through history (like the French Revolution) or the great and powerful individuals who stand in the midst of these forces and transform them (like Napoleon). When considering American Lutheran history, one can name any number of great and influential leaders, but the leader who put the most definitive stamp on his denomination would be clear; that man is C. F. W. Walther, the founding father of the Lutheran Church–Missouri Synod. Even after 200 years, Walther's legacy can clearly be seen, both in the denomination he founded and within the larger realm of American Lutheranism.

Carl Ferdinand Wilhelm Walther

Carl Ferdinand Wilhelm Walther was born October 25, 1811, in the German state of Saxony, the eighth of twelve children. His family included a number of prominent pastors going back several generations, and so he entered the University of Leipzig to study for the ministry, graduating in 1833. He was ordained in the Lutheran ministry in 1837. This was a time of considerable turmoil for Lutheranism; new intellectual and theological currents were pushing through Germany, as well as a conservative confessional reaction to them. After some personal turmoil, Walther found assurance of faith from a dynamic Lutheran pastor in Dresden, Martin Stephan. Stephan was in direct conflict with the government in Saxony over the religious direction of the state church (a concern that Walther shared), and when Stephan led a party of 665 emigrants to leave Germany in 1838, Walther was among them. This group arrived near St. Louis in 1839.

Walther was initially assigned as pastor to two small Lutheran congregations, but the whole colony was thrown into an uproar in May 1839 when Stephan was accused and then convicted of personal malfeasance, and was exiled from the colony. During the next two years Walther struggled to find his theological bearings within the turmoil from the Stephan affair, but by 1841 he had emerged as one of the leading theological voices within the colony and took a position as pastor of the first Lutheran congregation in St. Louis. From this base, Walther began to reach out to a wider Lutheran audience through a new publication, *Der Lutheraner*, founded in 1844, and through the establishment in 1847 of the German Evangelical Lutheran Synod of Missouri, Ohio, and Other States (now the Lutheran Church–Missouri Synod).

Though Walther only served as president of the new synod from 1847 to 1850 and later from 1864 to 1878, his personal influence on this group was strong, especially as editor of its newspaper, and on its theological journal, *Lehre und Wehre*, begun in 1855. But his primary platform was as professor at Concordia Seminary, St. Louis, where he taught from 1850 to the end of his life. From this position, Walther sought to influence the whole of American Lutheranism, and it was from here that he put his personal stamp on hundreds of young pastors who became the core of the newly-organized Missouri Synod, which rapidly grew to become one of the largest Lutheran denominations in the United States.

Walther at the organ

Walther clear represented and defined a form of deeply confessional Lutheranism that stood in opposition to many contemporary religious movements—against the theological liberalism found in Germany, against other forms of Protestantism found in North America, and against any form of American Lutheranism that seemed to him to have compromised with these other movements. Standing on a firm adherence to the Lutheran confessional documents found in the Book of Concord, 1580, Walther defined a strict, uncompromising Lutheranism, with a position that any cooperation between Lutheran groups must be founded on complete theological agreement. He strongly urged the formation of local parochial schools in Missouri Synod congregations as a means of maintaining and extending pure Lutheranism in America. He wrote a number of important theological works, but none more influential than *The Proper Distinction between Law and Gospel*, published in 1897, after his death.

The cover of Walther's influential volume

Walther was a strong leader and a strong personality. He attracted many pastors and congregations to join the Missouri Synod, but he also made enemies from within the leaders of other conservative Lutheran denominations, especially the leaders of the Ohio and Iowa Synods. In 1877, as a reaction against Walther's criticism of another Lutheran theologian's position on predestination, a bitter theological controversy erupted with Walther's own theological position at the center of the controversy. As a result, a number of these other Lutheran denominations pushed away from Missouri, which was left relatively isolated, though this did not stop Missouri's own internal growth. Walther died on May 7, 1887, acknowledged as the premier leader of the Missouri Synod and one of the most important figures in American Lutheran history.

MARK GRANQUIST

When Is a Lutheran Not a Lutheran?

The history of early Lutheranism in North America includes the story of a remarkable family of clergy. Paul Henkel and his sons and grandsons left an indelible mark on Lutheran church life for nearly a century, beginning in the mid-1700s.

Paul Henkel was born in North Carolina and served in the Revolutionary War. He and his sons, Samuel, Philip, Ambrose, Andrew, David and Charles, established a Lutheran printing establishment at New Market, Virginia, in the Shenandoah Valley.

Paul Henkel

The Henkels were unapologetic about championing the Augsburg Confession. The document, written by Martin Luther's teaching colleague Philip Melanchthon, was created to prove to emperor and pope that the Lutherans were authentic Christians, contrary to the claims of the Roman Catholic hierarchy in the 1500s. Once it became clear that Luther's reforms would be rejected by the church hierarchy of his day, the Augsburg Confession became the identifying document uniting Lutherans all over Europe.

The Henkels were determined that the same document should be similarly embraced by Lutherans in North America. From their press came Lutheran books and literature, including copies of Martin Luther's Catechism and the Augsburg Confession. Copies were circulated all over the regions where Lutherans had already settled—New York, Pennsylvania, Maryland, Virginia, North Carolina, Tennessee, Kentucky, Ohio, and Indiana.

The Henkels' devotion to the Augsburg Confession was not shared by all Lutherans in the American colonies and during the early national period of the young nation's history. In Pennsylvania, Lutheran and Reformed church congregations were creating "union churches," with two parishes sharing one pastor. For obvious reasons, the Lutheran confessional documents were downplayed. When the North Carolina Synod was organized in 1803, no reference was made to Lutheran confessional writings.

In the early 1800s, a prominent Pennsylvania pastor, Samuel Simon Schmucker, proposed uniting the several Lutheran synods into a national church body. Schmucker was on record supporting ecumenical relations with non-Lutheran groups. Schmucker felt a responsibility toward the German Lutheran congregations in Pennsylvania, many of which were involved in "union church" partnerships. He had no interest in forcing these communities to split apart.

The debate was joined. "How 'Lutheran' does a Lutheran really need to be?" Schmucker said, "Not so much as to get in the way of sharing ministry with other Christians." The Henkels said, "It's *very* important. Lutheranism offers valuable insights you can't get anywhere else. So don't water it down."

A songbook published by Henkel Press

In 1820, when Schmucker's General Synod appeared to be coming to fruition, the Henkels went into battle mode. They opposed the new national church structure because they didn't trust centralizing authority in the hands of a few people. And they didn't want the likes of Samuel Simon Schmucker exercising that authority.

Alarmed at the "confessional laxity" of the newly-created North Carolina Synod (which also supported the proposed General Synod), the Henkels worked to organize two new regional churches more committed to the Augsburg Confession. The Ohio Synod was organized in 1818, the Tennessee Synod in 1820. Neither became reliable supporters of the General Synod.

Long after Paul Henkel had died, Schmucker circulated a document in the General Synod proposing to revise the Augsburg

Confession, changing some of its articles. (The elder Henkel would have turned over in his grave.) For example, Schmucker wanted to redefine the meaning of Holy Communion. His proposed change to the Augsburg Confession would have discarded Martin Luther's insistence on Christ's "real presence" in the bread and wine, moving instead toward a Reformed understanding (declaring Christ is symbolically or spiritually present at the Eucharist). Schmucker's proposal went nowhere. Even his own synod in Pennsylvania voted against it.

Over the generations, the Henkels' point of view prevailed. Schmucker's program to Americanize Lutheranism was repudiated. The Augsburg Confession, without changes, was reaffirmed as a unifying document giving identity to Martin Luther's spiritual descendants. Part of the reason this became possible was that an increasing flood of new Lutheran immigrants continued to arrive from Europe—most of whom believed the Lutheran confessions were something worth championing. The Henkels were vindicated in their concern that Lutheranism should have a distinct identity.

The Henkel family continued to provide leadership for the growing American church into the third generation. Solomon's son, Samuel, became a physician but was also involved with translating and publishing standard Lutheran works for congregations. Philip's two sons, Ireneus and Eusebius, became Lutheran pastors in the western settlements. David's sons, Polycarp and Socrates, both became Lutheran clergy.

And the family left another legacy besides. Henkel Press was the earliest predecessor of what eventually became Fortress Press in Philadelphia and, since 1988, Augsburg Fortress Publishers in Minneapolis.

MICHAEL L. SHERER

William A. Passavant: Gospel Ranger

William A. Passavant's life (1821-94) provides a wide window into nineteenth-century American Lutheranism. In those years Lutherans were adapting themselves and their churches to the landscape of American Protestant Christianity. They debated about theology and religious practices. They reconsidered their alliances and reorganized church governance. They devised ways to meet their members' needs and serve their neighbors. Passavant had his hands on all of this.

He was born to German immigrants in Zeleinople, Pennsylvania. He lived in Pennsylvania most of his life, serving as pastor of Christ Lutheran in Baden for twenty-one years. However, his work and travels took him from Maryland to Minnesota. He ministered to the Americanized grandchildren of colonial German immigrants, to newly arrived Scandinavians, and to African-Americans. His ministry included preaching, teaching, publishing, and founding educational and charitable institutions.

William A. Passavant

In his twenties, Passavant left Gettysburg Seminary for Baltimore. Immediately he began editorial and pastoral work, a combination he continued elsewhere. Along with his responsibilities at the *Lutheran Observer,* he conducted neighborhood evangelistic meetings and organized Sunday schools. He not only gathered scattered Lutherans, but also preached to new audiences. Each day he read German to improve his ability to reach immigrants. The loud, extravagant response he received from African-Americans required him to adjust his style. Founding congregations was the next step. After six busy months he was invited to stay permanently.

The young pastor, however, had other ambitions, which he expressed in a letter to his mother:

... the idea of sitting down in one spot and becoming as other ministers, having the same round of duties from week to week and year to year, is to me now as it always has been very melancholy. You may think me foolish on these subjects, and perhaps I am, but my feelings are unchanged on these matters. I have always longed to be a gospel ranger, to go from place to place assisting my companions in labor, or laying a foundation on which others might build.

His feelings on these matters remained unchanged for five decades during which he left his mark in many places.

In his youth he was influenced by the so-called American Lutheranism at Gettysburg Seminary. He admired John Wesley and was eager for revival. By mid-century his views aligned with the moderate Confessionalists who established a seminary in Philadelphia and founded the General Council. When the Definite Synodical Platform (with its call for corrections to the Augsburg Confession) ignited heated conflict, Passavant took sides even as he tried to calm the flames. He was persuaded to expand his magazine, *The Missionary*, to a weekly that provided an English outlet for the moderates.

Passavant used *The Missionary* to promote mission work in the western territories and abroad. He raised funds for specific efforts and appealed for workers. Nonetheless, joining his publication with *The Lutheran* in 1861 freed him for his other activities, particularly mission and mercy. These two he regarded as the central work of the church. He advocated for city missions and also traveled to rural settlements. Passavant encouraged and modeled collaboration between English-speaking Lutherans and new immigrants. He was a friend and trusted advisor to pastors, such as the Swedish leader Eric Norelius in Minnesota.

In 1846 Passavant represented the Pittsburgh Synod at the Christian Alliance convention in London. He also visited Germany. In Kaiserswerth, Theodore Fliedner introduced him to the deaconess institute and its associated programs. Back in the United States, Passavant set about replicating several of them. The Pittsburgh Infirmary (later Passavant Hospital) opened in 1849. It was the first Protestant hospital in the nation. Four deaconesses sent from Germany were on its staff. Passavant also helped found hospitals in Chicago and Jacksonville, Illinois, and in Milwaukee, Wisconsin, as well as several orphanages. This work continues, both through local institutions and in Lutheran Social Service organizations.

From his student days, Passavant was involved in education as an extension of faith and for the preparation of leaders. Thiel College (now in Greenville, Pennsylvania) counts him among its founders. He supported the seminary in Philadelphia and was involved in starting another in Chicago to serve the church as it expanded westward. When the General Council took up this proposal in the late 1860s the

The Hospital Passavant founded in Milwaukee began in a farm house (above) and later developed into a primary medical facility for Milwaukee residents (below).

delegates expressed their hope — and Passavant's — that the school would educate pastoral candidates for all the churches.

The seminary opened in 1891. Its charter stipulated that the school would: "*Educate Together*, men of a pure faith, of a holy life and of the requisite gifts and education, so that by all necessary learning and practical skill, they may be fitted for the ministry of the gospel, especially in connection with the Evangelical Lutheran Church." In other words, its goal was to raise up leaders to build on the foundations Passavant laid.

L. DEANE LAGERQUIST

The Apostolic Lutheran Tradition

Apostolic or Laestadian Lutheranism, with its roots in the nineteenth century revival of northern Scandinavia and Finland, remains arguably the most enigmatic aspect of North American Lutheranism. The small size of this heritage coupled with the social isolation that is found among at least some of its congregations has caused many to overlook these Finnish-ethnic Lutheran groups.

Lars Levi Laestadius

Like other branches of American Lutheranism, Apostolic Lutheranism traces its roots to Pietistic awakening movements that swept across Europe from the seventeenth to the nineteenth centuries. The awakening movement in question was led by Lars Levi Laestadius (1800-1861), a pastor in the State Church (Lutheran) of Sweden. Sometimes called the "Prophet of Lapland," Laestadius carried out his ministry in the region north of the Arctic Circle where Finland, Norway, and Sweden share borders. Therefore, the revival movement that bore his name influenced all of these Nordic countries to some extent, though it was in Finland that Laestadian influence took root most deeply.

In 1826, Laestadius received an appointment as the pastor of a remote parish in the Swedish Lapland. Though there was a spirit of stagnation in this parish regarding spiritual matters, Laestadius was not overly-concerned. In addition to theology, he had an interest in botany, and some commentators remark that his passion for the study of plants exceeded his passion for the gospel of Jesus Christ. He would come to understand later that what he taught during that time had more to do with "head knowledge" than with Christian conviction.

As Laestadius became seriously ill for the second time in his life in 1842, he reflected on his eternal destiny. His illness caused him to recognize his poverty of spirit and the same ungodliness that existed within his parish. Upon his recovery, he began to emphasize what others would call "living Christianity," something that moved beyond a focus on doctrine and morals. For Laestadius, it is not enough to simply try to be a better person; what truly produces Christian people is the recognition that their emptiness can only be filled with the righteousness of Christ. Laestadius' new kind of preaching caught on in the Lapland, from which many thirsty souls drank deeply.

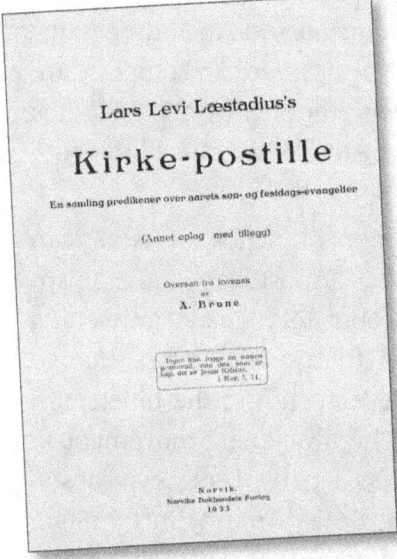

To this day, there are Lutherans in the Nordic countries that identify with the tradition of Laestadius. Due to Laestadius' emphasis on the need for a public recounting of sins. Laestadians in these countries are known for some peculiar regulations that organize their lives, such as a refusal to use curtains in homes so as to avoid engaging in secret sins. As immigration fever swept across Europe in the nineteenth century, Laestadians were among the many Europeans who sought a new home in North America for a variety of reasons.

Like other Lutherans, Laestadians in America could no longer rely on the state churches of their home countries. The roots of what would become known as "Apostolic Lutheranism" began in Calumet, Michigan, with the founding of a congregation in 1873. An official church body would not be formed, however, until 1928. As more Finnish immigrants came to America, the Laestadians among them formed congregations that are concentrated in Michigan, northern Minnesota, and Washington. Today, most American Laestadians are found within two denominational groups, the Apostolic Lutheran Church of America and the Laestadian Lutheran Church, though many other, smaller bodies exist, as well as independent congregations.

Space does not permit a full discussion of the matters of doctrine and practice that have caused this small group of Lutherans to fragment in so many directions. Suffice it to say that some Apostolic Lutheran congregations are more open to the modern world and resemble American evangelicalism. Other congregations are isolationist in their outlook and have been affectionately labeled "Lutheran Amish" due to their non-conformity in matters of dress and their discouragement of higher education. In spite of some peculiar theological emphases among certain Apostolic Lutherans, they do clearly fall within the boundaries of historic Lutheran teaching. Curiously, however, some groups of Apostolics claim that they are the only real Christians in the world, their form of "living Christianity" being the only legitimate form of Christian expression, a belief that has led some to label such groups of Apostolic Lutherans as "cults."

Perhaps in time a greater understanding will be reached between Apostolic Lutherans and other branches of Lutheranism in North America. Such would require intentional engagement with the leadership of these many and varied communities. Until then, the best source of information about Apostolic Lutheranism comes in a book by Carl A. Kulla: *The Journey of an Immigrant Awakening Movement in America: A Brief History of Laestadianism and the Apostolic Lutheran Church*. For more information about Lars Levi Laestadius himself, see chapter eight of *They Lived in the Power of God: Lutheran Revival Leaders in Northern Europe*.

THOMAS JACOBSON

Samuel Simon Schmucker and the General Synod

He was, if nothing else, an ambitious young man, with a vision of truly American Lutheranism. At the time of his birth in 1799, the new American republic was growing and expanding, with a sense of incurable optimism, vibrant energy, and unlimited horizons. Samuel Simon Schmucker (1799-1873) embodied this new American spirit in his untiring work for the consolidation and expansion of Lutheranism in North America. From a very young age, Schmucker played a prominent role, not only in American Lutheranism, but also in the wider world of Anglo-American Protestantism. No stranger to controversy, he was admired by many and detested by others, but he left an indelible mark on his church and his age.

Samuel Simon Schmucker

A third-generation American Lutheran, Schmucker was born in 1799 into an extended Lutheran clerical family. Intelligent and precocious, he studied theology first with his father, then at Princeton Theological Seminary (there being no Lutheran seminary at the time). He was ordained at age twenty-one and began serving Lutheran congregations in Virginia. Concerned for Lutheran ministerial education, the (very) young Schmucker set up a proto-seminary in his parsonage, personally training a number of clergy candidates, among all his other duties.

Although by the early 1820s the geographical expansion of American Lutheranism had resulted in the formation of six regional synods, there was no national organization to coordinate their efforts or expand Lutheranism further. In 1820 the attempt was made to form a General Synod to meet this need, but in 1823 opposition and infighting among American Lutherans imperiled this fledgling institution. Though he was dealing with the painful loss of his own young wife, Schmucker swung into action and through dozens of letters and personal contacts, along with coordinating his family's efforts, he managed to save the nascent General Synod from collapse. For the next fifty years, Schmucker would be its leading figure.

In 1826 the General Synod was able to form the first permanent Lutheran seminary, at Gettysburg, Pennsylvania. Schmucker was, of course, instrumental in the formation of this seminary and was elected the first (and only) professor of this institution; he was twenty-six. For the next thirty-eight years he would put his personal stamp on the institution and on North American Lutheranism, though his education and preparation of some 400 Lutheran pastors and through the publication of over 40 books, including an influential theological textbook, a handbook for synodical and congregation organization, and a number of polemical works.

The Gettysburg Gymnasium, the first college building

This period of time was both formative and divisive for American Lutheran theology. Many Lutherans were drawn to the dominant Reformed or Revivalistic Protestantism, some leaned toward Deism, while still others, reacting against these trends, pushed for strict Lutheran confessionalism. Schmucker tried to forge a centrist pathway for American Lutherans in the midst of these diverging tendencies. Against the strict and separatist Lutherans, Schmucker insisted that Lutheran confessionalism ought to be open enough to allow contacts and influences from the wider Protestant world.

In the 1850s, as a part of this vision of an expansive and ecumenical Lutheranism, Schmucker and others offered, anonymously at first, a new American revision of the Lutheran theological standard, the Augsburg Confession. Convinced that the only way to "save" this confessional document for American Lutheran was to modify it theologically at several places where it did not fit current American Lutheran practice, they did so. Schmucker and his allies believed that Augsburg's maintenance of doctrines such as baptismal regeneration and the real presence was a medieval Catholic holdover, ideas that American Lutherans no longer held (which, in the majority, they probably did not). The only way to maintain the authority of the Augsburg Confession (which Schmucker did believe in) was to bring it into conformity with contemporary American Lutheran sensitivities.

Samuel Simon Schmucker

However well intentioned, this attempt was a failure, and it cost the unity of his beloved General Synod. Conservative Lutherans outside the General Synod went ballistic over Schmucker's attempt to modify the Augsburg Confession and saw in it the proof that the General Synod had completely forfeited its Lutheran heritage. More ominously, Schmucker's proposed American edition also created unrest within important sections of the General Synod itself and among some of Schmucker's former students, a number of whom were now important theological leaders. The ensuing controversy over Schmucker's American Lutheranism resulted eventually in a split in the General Synod; the withdrawal of several constituent synods and the eventual formation, in 1867, of a rival national organization of Lutheran synods, the General Council.

Schmucker's legacy in American Lutheranism is complicated and contested. Some Lutherans see him as a symbol of all the things in American Lutheranism that they do not like. Others see in him a vision of ecumenical Christian openness that they admire. Regardless, his influence is rooted deeply in a Lutheranism in America that he was instrumental in forming.

MARK GRANQUIST

African-American Lutherans

On Palm Sunday 1669 a Lutheran pastor in Albany, New York, baptized into his congregation an African-American man who was given the name Emmanuel. In subsequent years other African-Americans, enslaved or free, became members of Lutheran congregations in New York and New Jersey. Thus there have been African-American Lutherans in this country for over 350 years, longer than many of the other groups of European immigrants we generally think of as being Lutheran.

African-Americans became Lutherans in many places in the colonial period; besides New York they were found in the Carolinas and Georgia, on the Danish Virgin Islands, and in British and Dutch Guiana in South America. Though not always, they often were slaves of Lutheran masters. Initially, Lutherans were against slavery, but some quickly adapted to it in this country. By the time of the Civil War, there were several thousand African-American Lutheran members in the South, and many more (probably 8,000-10,000) who had been baptized Lutheran. In 1832 an African-American Lutheran preacher named Jehu Jones formed St. Paul's Colored Lutheran Church in Philadelphia, which survived until 1849. Another African-American Lutheran, Daniel Payne, graduated from Gettysburg Seminary in 1837. After some years as a Lutheran pastor he became a bishop in the African Methodist Episcopal Church.

Jehu Jones

Daniel Payne

After the Civil War, most of the African-American Lutherans in the South left the white congregations, where they generally had been second-class citizens. In response, various southern Lutheran synods began sporadic efforts to evangelize the newly-freed African-Americans and to build separate Lutheran congregations. Starting in 1868, the Lutheran synods in Tennessee, North Carolina, South Carolina, and Georgia licensed African-American preachers to preach the gospel and gather congregations. These efforts were poorly funded at best, and in 1889 (out of desperation) the African-American preachers in the North Carolina Synod formed the Alpha Synod, the first African-American Lutheran church organization. This little synod, and the other African-American Lutheran congregations in the South, struggled for survival through the end of the nineteenth century.

As national Lutheran denominations formed in the nineteenth century, they began to do mission work outside their own ethnic boundaries. Many times this meant foreign missions, but it also meant to some evangelism among minority groups in the United States. In 1877 the Synodical Conference (dominated by the Lutheran Church–Missouri Synod) began mission work among African-Americans, first in Little Rock and then more successfully in New Orleans. Subsequently, the Synodical Conference also incorporated the preachers and congregations of the Alpha Synod, and they began a very successful mission work among African-Americans in Alabama (where they were joined by the Joint Synod of Ohio). In the South these African-American Lutherans opened schools, academies, and teacher-training institutions, one of which grew into Concordia College, Selma, Alabama, the only historically-black Lutheran college in the country.

Beginning around World War I, the "Great Migration" of African Americans to the cities of the North and West brought new African-American Lutheran congregations in these cities, thirty-eight of them founded between 1923 and 1950. Some of these congregations were formed by migrants from the American south, while others were composed of immigrants from the Virgin Islands and from South America. By 1950, there were nearly 11,000 African-American Lutherans, mostly in urban areas.

With the Civil Rights movement, beginning in the 1950s, the old era of African-American Lutheranism began to change. Prior to this most Lutheran congregations were segregated, but beginning in the 1960s the three American Lutheran denominations began to push for integrated congregations and increased outreach to African Americans. In the Lutheran Church in America, the number of African-American members jumped from 5,000 in 1962 to 49,000 in

1989 (with 111 African-American pastors), when the LCA became a part of the ELCA. In all the American Lutheran bodies in 1991, there were 132,000 African American Lutherans (about two percent of all Lutherans). In the last twenty years, new Lutheran immigrants from Africa have formed a number of congregations around the country.

How should these numbers be seen? They are, in part, a success story, but they also indicate that had white Lutherans been more consistently supportive of African-American Lutherans, these numbers could have been much higher. African-American Lutherans have often heroically struggled to build and maintain their congregations, only occasionally assisted by white Lutherans. Their accomplishments must be honored and their 350 year legacy lifted up.

MARK GRANQUIST

Daniel Payne and Jehu Jones: African-Americans and Lutheranism

History is sometimes quite a bit messier than we know. The situation of African-Americans in the South before the Civil War was not the same for all, and especially in the southern cities there was a sizable population of African-Americans who had earned their freedom. They still faced harsh discrimination and great poverty, but these free blacks were able to have some control over their own lives, and some of them were able, despite the odds, to become leaders. This is the story of two such free men from Charleston, South Carolina— Daniel Payne and Jehu Jones, who were the first two African-Americans ordained by Lutherans in the United States. Though they came out of a similar situation, their stories diverged rather dramatically.

These stories begin at a Lutheran congregation, St. John's Lutheran in Charleston, South Carolina, and its pastor, the Rev. John Bachman. Bachman was quite an accomplished and enigmatic figure. A prominent Lutheran leader and renowned naturalist, he gathered a large African-American congregation at St. John's, while also being a staunch defender of slavery. The African-American congregation there consisted of both enslaved and free blacks, and was quite active up to the Civil War. It was from this congregation that both Jones and Payne were sent into the ministry. But the similarities between the two men end at this point.

John Bachman

Jehu Jones was a free black man living in Charleston, where he was a successful tradesman and a member of the black congregation at St. John's since the early 1820s. He was definitely a leader in that congregation, though to describe him so at the time was controversial. In 1832 the St. John's congregation decided that it wanted to send an African-American as a missionary to the country of Liberia, then

Jehu Jones

being colonized by black Americans returning to Africa. They decided that Jones should go, and he agreed. Jones went to New York to seek assistance for his mission to Africa, and though nothing came of his requests, he did make connections with the Lutheran Ministerium in New York. Because as an African-American Jones could not be ordained by Lutherans in the South, he was ordained by members of the New York Ministerium in 1832, becoming the first black person ordained as a Lutheran pastor. After several years of frustration, Jones had to abandon the idea of this mission to Liberia. Moving his family several times around the cities in the American North, Jones supported them working as a tailor. Finally, in 1834, Jones settled in Philadelphia, where there was a sizeable African-American community. Inspired by the presence of several large African-American congregations in that city, in the same year Jones organized the St. Paul's Colored Lutheran Church of Philadelphia, the first independent African-American Lutheran congregation in the United States (or perhaps the world). Though the congregation met regularly and began to build a church building, it soon encountered major financial difficulties. Jones appealed to Lutheran leaders for financial assistance and did receive some, but the congregation went out of existence in 1839. Undeterred, Jones continued his efforts, and in 1849 appealed to the New York Ministerium for assistance in opening an African-American Lutheran congregation in New York. His request was denied, and we do not know anything more of Jehu Jones after that point.

Although the building is no longer standing, the cornerstone for St. paul's Colored Lutheran Church has been preserved.

The career of Daniel Payne was quite a bit different. He became a very successful educator and church leader, although not in the Lutheran church. Like Jones, Payne was a free black man in Charleston. Largely self-educated, Payne organized several very successful schools for African-Americans in Charleston, which were closed in

1835 by the passage of a law forbidding such schools. Though Payne was not a Lutheran, he was encouraged by Pastor Bachman to go to New York City, where a mission organization gave him the funding for further education. In 1837 Payne enrolled at the Lutheran Seminary in Gettysburg, Pennsylvania, where he studied for two years, until health problems ended his education there. In 1837 Payne was ordained by the Franckean Synod, an abolitionist Lutheran synod in New York, but he never served a Lutheran congregation. For several years he taught school and occasionally served as pastor, until in 1841 he became a pastor in the African Methodist Episcopal Church (AME). Because of his intellect and leadership skills, Payne quickly achieved prominence in this African-American denomination, being ordained as a bishop in 1852. In 1863 he became president of Wilberforce University in Ohio, an AME college, where he served for many years. He was a distinguished leader in the African-American community until his death in 1893.

Daniel Payne

Wilberforce University in 1856, the first private, historically African-American university in the United States

These two important African-Americans had early connections to American Lutheranism, but led very different lives.

MARK GRANQUIST

The Clash at Koshkonong: Eielsen and Dietrichson

Given their commitments and their temperaments, it was inevitable that they would quickly come into conflict. Though these two young pastors were from Norway, and ministering to Norwegian immigrants settling in Wisconsin in the 1840s, these two men were as different as could be. Elling Eielsen was a low-church lay preacher out of the Hauge revival movement in Norway, whereas J. W. C. Dietrichson was a university-trained state church pastor, committed to the order and ritual of the Church of Norway. When they met, they clashed, but in their conflict they set the parameters for a vibrant Norwegian-American Lutheranism that put down deep roots in North America.

First on the scene was Elling Eielsen. A fiery lay evangelist in Scandinavia, in 1839 he was forced to come to America to continue his work. Following in the mold of the Pietist leader Hans Nielsen Hauge, Eielsen pushed for a strict, moral Christian life and a commitment to a deeply personal Christian faith, things that he saw lacking in the congregations and the pastors of the Lutheran Church of Norway. Though he wished to remain a lay preacher in the United States, he soon saw the need for ordination to fully serve the immigrant communities, and he was ordained in 1843. Dietrichson arrived at bit later, in 1844. He was an aristocratic young man, university trained and "properly" ordained by a bishop into the ministry of the Church of Norway. He was deeply committed to the formal Lutheran theology and ritual of the state church, with a high view of theology and ministry. Both men have been described as stubborn, passionate, and tactless, and the clash between them was inevitably explosive.

Elling Eielsen

After Dietrichson arrived in America in 1844, he soon took over the Lutheran congregation at Koshkonong, Wisconsin. Seeing himself a more than just a pastor, but as carrying the authority of the Church of Norway in this new country, he soon set out to create a "proper" Norwegian Lutheranism in North America, under his guidance. One of his first targets was Eielsen, who had already gathered together a string of Norwegian congregations and preaching points in Wisconsin and Illinois. A meeting was arranged between these two young pastors which, of course, did not go well. The aristocratic Dietrichson took it upon himself to challenge Eielsen's lack of education and the validity of his ordination. As to the challenge about his training and ministerial examination, Eielsen retorted that he had been called by God and examined as had been the apostles, by "persecution, wakefulness, nakedness, and hunger." Eielsen detested almost everything that Dietrichson stood for, and when Dietrichson pronounced that Eielsen's ordination was invalid, Eielsen hotly lashed out, grabbed Dietrichson by the beard, and exclaimed, "Listen to me, you pope, I intend to plague you as long as I live." So much for intra-Lutheran cooperation.

J. W. C. Dietrichson

Actually, neither of these two pioneer pastors had successful, long-term careers in North America. Dietrichson never achieved the kind of leadership he imagined in America and returned to Norway around 1850, where he had similar problems with local Norwegian congregations. Eielsen remained in America until his death in 1883, but he alienated many of the Norwegian-American Lutherans, and the church organization that he founded remained a small player within American Lutheranism. This said, it is clear that both Dietrichson and Eielsen were still very important figures in Norwegian-American Lutheranism, as each of them symbolically defined both the parameters and the limits of this movement. These two pastors represented two wings of Lutheranism in nineteenth-century Norway—the warm lay pietism of the Hauge movement and the educated, formal Lutheranism of the state church. But beyond their personal foibles, these two pastors also demonstrated the limits of transplanting these traditions into North America. Hauge Pietism was a movement in

Norway, but in North America it had to become a church and take on some of those churchly trappings that it had always resisted. Similarly, state church Lutheranism of the Norwegian variety also could not be directly transplanted into North America, but took on both Pietist and American features.

Norwegian-American Lutheranism grew rapidly and developed a rich series of traditions and structures, all within the limits initially set out by Eielsen and Dietrichson, but also creatively adapting its Norwegian traditions and to its North American context. The vitality of these Norwegian-American Lutherans often verged into conflict, but they also creatively developed a tradition of churchly Pietism, between the two extremes. This Lutheranism drew from both positions in a creative manner that was appropriate to the immigrants and their children, and which was also definitely American. It was also very successful. By 1960 Norwegian-American Lutherans numbered over one million members. Not bad, considering the somewhat rocky beginnings!

MARK GRANQUIST

Father Adam Keffer and Early Canadian Lutheranism

How far would you go to get a pastor? Would you walk 500 miles (round trip) in blustery spring weather, and do it not only once, but twice? This sounds like an impossible undertaking, but it really happened in 1849 and 1850, when Adam Keffer, a lay leader of some Lutherans near Toronto, walked twice to Pennsylvania in order to find a Lutheran pastor for his congregation. On top of it all, "Father" Keffer was over sixty years old!

German Lutherans started coming to Canada in the eighteenth century. There were Lutheran congregations started in Nova Scotia in the 1750s, which were reinforced by "Loyalist" American Lutherans who went north during the Revolutionary War. In 1793, a group of 350 Germans Lutherans, who had originally settled in New York, crossed the Great Lakes and founded settlements in Ontario, outside of Toronto. They had been unable to find land in New York and accepted a generous offer from the governor in Ontario for 64,000 acres.

This area was wilderness; the group had great trouble reaching the area and further trouble in settling there. But they persevered and founded a number of small Lutheran congregations. These Lutherans had brought a pastor along with them, but he remained with them for only a few years, then returned to Germany. After this, the fledgling congregations were occasionally served by regular Lutheran pastors, but there were long periods of vacancy in between.

In early North America, there were never enough pastors to go around, and this was especially true on the frontier. In desperation, congregations often had to resort to whatever kinds of pastors they could find, and there were many imposters running around claiming to be pastors when they really were not. Carl Cronmiller, an historian of Canadian Lutheranism, wrote, "These men may be described as clerical tramps, some of who were discharged Army officers or schoolteachers, imposters who pretended to be ordained clergymen." These early Canadian Lutherans suffered from abuse at the hands of several such irregular pastors, who almost destroyed their congregations. In desperation, some Lutheran congregations were lured away and joined the Anglican church.

A stained glass representation of Father Adam Keffer, carrying his shoes, in the History Window at St. Peter's Church, Ottawa, Ontario, Canada

In 1849, some of the remaining members of Zion Lutheran Church, Maple, Ontario, sent one of their elders, Adam Keffer, to the United States to find a pastor for them. Keffer was the son of one of the original founders of the congregation, and at the time he was over sixty years old. Keffer set out walking for Pennsylvania and, tradition has it, carried his shoes most of the way (to save them from getting worn out). Eventually Keffer was directed to a meeting of a new Lutheran organization, the Pittsburgh Synod, which was meeting in the spring of 1849 in Klecknerville, Pennsylvania. One of the members of the synod, the Rev. William Passavant, discovered Father Keffer walking barefoot in a garden at the edge of the village and invited to the synodical meeting. Once at the meeting, Keffer gave an impassioned appeal to the group for a pastor and for financial assistance.

The young Pittsburgh Synod (only four years old) sent one of its pastors to Ontario that summer to survey the field, but there was

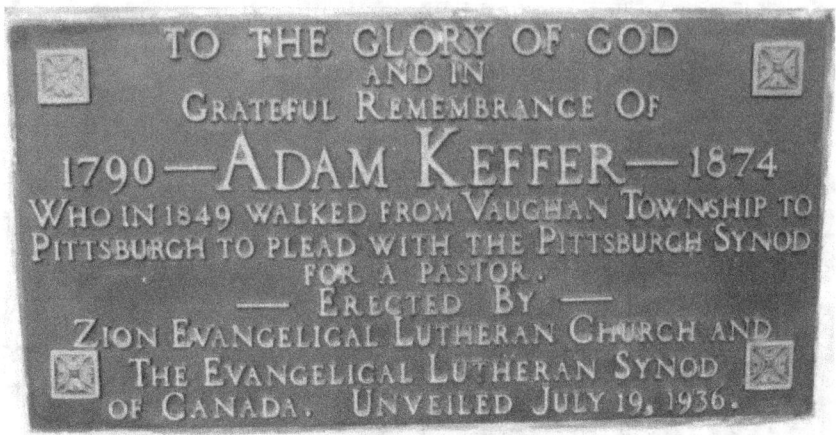

A monument to Keffer at Zion Lutheran Church in Vaughn Township, Canada, recalling his long walk to plead for a pastor

no immediate aid for the Canadian Lutherans beyond this. The next year, in the spring of 1850, the Pittsburgh Synod met in Pittsburgh, and, to the astonishment of all, Adam Keffer showed up again, having walked over 250 miles to reach the meeting. He delivered the same impassioned pleas as the year before and this time got results. As the synodical newspaper, *The Missionary*, records it: "The interviews of this aged patriarch with the Synod, and his agonizing entreaties for someone to come over and help them, went to the heart of everyone, and awakened an interest for the mission cause never before felt."

This time Father Keffer's prayers were answered, and a series of Lutheran pastors from the Pittsburgh Synod began long and successful ministries in Ontario. In the next decade, several dozen congregations were reactivated or formed. By 1853 these congregations in Ontario were organized into the Canada Conference of the Pittsburgh Synod, an event which marks the first Lutheran synodical organization in Canada itself and the oldest forerunner of the current Evangelical Lutheran Church in Canada.

All this was possible because one old man would not stand by and see his congregation die for lack of a good pastor. In current language you could say that he "walked the walk" as well as "talked the talk."

MARK GRANQUIST

Elisabeth Fedde, Founder of Norwegian-American Lutheran Deaconess Movement

As a young woman in Norway, Elisabeth Fedde felt a strong desire for a life of service, but when a friend suggested that she consider deaconess work, she replied, "Do you mean those women we see on the streets wearing peculiar dress? No thank you. I shall not join them." Later, when she learned more about the diaconal mission—to serve God by serving others—she decided to apply. In 1873, she entered the Deaconess House in Kristiania (Oslo) and began two years of training in nursing, Christian ethics, and social welfare. There she began twenty-seven years of active service as a deaconess, service that brought her to America to serve the Norwegian immigrants.

Elisabeth Fedde

On Christmas 1882, following a difficult four-year assignment in Tromsø in the far north, Sister Elisabeth received a letter from her brother-in-law, Gabriel Fedde, asking her to come to Brooklyn to begin deaconess work "here among the poor and lost Norwegians." Responding to this plea, Sister Elisabeth arrived in New York in April 1883, knowing no English and without any Norwegian sponsorship. Within nine days she helped establish the Voluntary Relief Society for the Sick and Poor Among Norwegians in New York and Brooklyn with a mission "to help the poor and suffering countrymen and women in their spiritual and bodily need"—the beginning of Norwegian Lutheran Deaconess work in America.

There was plenty of need, not only in homes and overcrowded hospitals, but also on ships in the harbor and out in the streets. The immigrant community suffered from disease, unemployment, alcohol abuse, overcrowded housing, and the struggle to adapt to a strange culture. Sister Elisabeth's diary records the broad scope of her work in those years. She made hundreds of home visits where, in addition to nursing and maternity care, she often cleaned and laundered. She spent hours soliciting and distributing money and essentials, placed patients in hospitals, arranged for burials, visited prisons, found foster care, tried to locate employment, and offered much needed spiritual support. Frequently exhausted and discouraged, she called on her deep faith to give her strength to continue.

Sister Elisabeth found so much need that she soon persuaded leaders of the Relief Society to start a hospital and deaconess home. By March 1885 she and a board of managers had rented a house in Brooklyn with room for a nine-bed hospital and living quarters for herself and other deaconesses, although it was soon clear that a larger hospital was needed.

First Brooklyn Hospital, with Sister Elisabeth Fedde at bottom of the stairs (in uniform), 1885

In 1888 Sister Elisabeth interrupted her work in Brooklyn to help begin deaconess work in Minneapolis. She was contacted by Professor Sven Oftedal and others who hoped to establish a deaconess hospital in Minneapolis. One generous donor offered a house free for two years if she would stay to organize the work and equip the hospital and deaconess home. Granted her a leave by her board, she agreed to accept the challenge. On November 2, 1888, she and two probationers moved into the home and a few days later opened a hospital in four rooms.

In 1889 Sister Elisabeth was called back to Brooklyn.

Fedde with Minneapolis deaconesses

Within months of her departure, the Minneapolis venture fell apart. She returned that summer to find that the hospital board had disbanded and work was at a standstill. At her urging, Professor Georg Sverdrup of Augsburg Seminary organized a new board, and in August 1889 the Norwegian Lutheran Deaconess Institute incorporated. By the end of 1889 there were eight sisters. But new trouble lay ahead. In 1891, after a dispute with her board, Sister Elisabeth resigned and returned to Brooklyn to resume her position there. This time the work in Minneapolis continued and thrived. The board bought new property for a larger home and hospital, and by 1899 the Deaconess Institute had eleven deaconess and twenty probationers. At its peak in 1912 there were fifty-two sisters.

In Brooklyn, a thirty-bed Deaconess Hospital was built in 1889. Sister Elisabeth called it "the first charitable institution among our people in America." The need for funding continued to be crucial. In 1894 Sister Elisabeth secured a $4,000 annual state subsidy for the Brooklyn hospital by appealing to a committee of the state legislature in Albany where she had argued that Deaconess Hospital served all nationalities and creeds and deserved to receive the same funding as other community hospitals.

Norwegian Lutheran Deaconess Hospital in Brooklyn, 1889

Weary and needing rest, Sister Elisabeth resigned from the Brooklyn Deaconess Hospital and returned to Norway in 1896 where she married Ole Slettebø. While there was still work to be done, in only thirteen years her determination and bold leadership had built the Norwegian Lutheran Deaconess community in America and helped to found two major hospitals, one in Brooklyn and the other in Minneapolis.

SUSAN COREY EVERSON

Danes Enriched the Mix

Denmark is a small country and, compared to other immigrant waves, Lutherans arriving in the U.S. from Denmark were a small group. But like salt and spice that improve the flavor of already good food, the Danes in America had a salutary effect.

There were lots of Lutherans, European immigrants all, who were already in North America when the Danes began arriving. Their big migration came in the late 1800s. Between 1851 and 1860, 3,749 Danish Lutherans arrived in North America. In the following decade there were 17,094; in the next ten years, 31,771; then came the flood, between 1881-1890, when 88,132 arrived.

Where did they go? Mostly to the Upper Midwest—Michigan, Wisconsin, Illinois, Iowa, Nebraska and Minnesota. And when they came, the Danes brought along two kinds of baggage, cultural and theological.

Like other ethnic Lutheran groups, they were keen to preserve Danish culture as best they could. That led, among other things, to the establishment of a half-dozen very successful "Folk Schools."

Students at the Solvang, California, Folk School

Lutheran sensibilities and Danish culture thrived in these resident, non-academic establishments, founded at Grant, Michigan; Elk Horn, Iowa; Nysted, Nebraska; Solvang, California; Dalum, Alberta, Canada; and Tyler, Minnesota.

None of the Folk Schools survive, although the school at Elk Horn, Iowa, contributed to the founding and growth of Dana College in

Blair, Nebraska. The demise of the Folk Schools was due to the same dynamic that led to the decline of Norwegian Lutheran academies (there were once fifty of them in Wisconsin alone) and German Lutheran parochial schools in predecessor ELCA church bodies. As Lutheran ethnic groups Americanized themselves, they stopped trying to look like carbon copies of their European forebears.

The theological energies that came to North America with the Danes were of two types, and they accounted for an early split in the Danish ranks. Some immigrants were enamored of the influence of the great Danish churchman N. S. Grundtvig, a powerful preacher, prolific hymn writer, and in many ways a highly unconventional theologian. (He seemed to attribute more authority to the Apostles' Creed than to Holy Scripture, which he said was not "the Word of God" but, instead, "contained" God's Word.)

N. S. Grundtvig

Grundtvig's theology caused consternation for a great many Danes who identified themselves with the "Inner Mission" movement and were, consequently, more inclined to embrace the impulses of Pietism. This European-born emphasis stressed spiritual change and tended to identify true religion with outward behavior, including purity of life. Pietism sometimes led to revival meetings, the encouraging of conversion experiences, staying off the dance floor, and a lifestyle that demonstrated godly living.

Two groups that championed Inner Mission sensibilities combined to create what became the United Evangelical Lutheran Church (UELC). At Blair, Nebraska, they founded Trinity Lutheran Seminary and, a few years later on the same campus, Dana College. This branch of the American Danish church came to be known as the "Holy Danes" (for obvious reasons). While Pietism accomplished impressive things, among Lutherans both in Europe and North America (one historian argues that all U.S. Lutheran groups were founded by pietists), it demanded a rigorous lifestyle that for some in the Danish church was the wrong approach.

Those Danes within the Grundtvigian movement organized themselves into what came to be known as the American Evangelical Lutheran Church (AELC). Their center became Des Moines, Iowa, where their seminary was founded and, shortly thereafter, Grand View College (now Grand View University). By choice or by accident, they came to be known as the "Happy Danes."

The UELC, anticipating a coming merger with Germans and Norwegians into the "new" American Lutheran Church (there was also an "old" ALC), closed Trinity Seminary in the late 1950s and sent its faculty, students, and library to Wartburg Theological Seminary in Dubuque, Iowa. In 1960, the ALC was created through a merger of the (Norwegian) Evangelical Lutheran Church, the (German) American Lutheran Church, and the UELC. It was, it should be noted, at the prompting of UELC leaders that the merger negotiations actually began.

A few years later the AELC merged with the (German) United Lutheran Church in America and the (Swedish) Augustana Synod. Grand View Seminary was merged with Maywood Seminary, as was Augustana Seminary, to create the Lutheran School of Theology at Chicago. The combining denominations took the name Lutheran Church in America (LCA). In 1988, when the ALC and the LCA became the ELCA, the two Danish Lutheran denominations in the U.S. finally ended up in the same church family.

Old Main, Dana College

A sad footnote to the Danish Lutheran story in this country is that in the middle of the first decade of this new century, Dana College, seriously short of funds, was forced to close its doors. That leaves Grand View University as the institutional reminder of the Danish Lutheran presence in North America.

MICHAEL L. SHERER

Education for Lutheran Children

Ole Oleson lived with his wife Bergit, two sons, and three daughters near Lake Johanna in Pope County, Minnesota, in 1880. The three girls were enrolled in public school. Gottlib Schmidt lived with his wife Threasa, and their six children in New Ulm in 1895; their children were in school too, but probably in a parochial school.

Four and a half million immigrants came from Germany or the countries that constituted Germany in the last half of the nineteenth century, and nearly one and a half million immigrants came from the Scandinavian countries of Sweden, Denmark, and Finland in the same time frame. The 392 Ole Olesons and the 6,432 Schmidts in Minnesota in the late nineteenth century had choices in where they sent their children. Those choices were there partly because of the cultural background they brought and partly because of the speed with which they integrated into their new country.

The Germans tended to include Lutheran elementary schools when they started a parish; the Scandinavians were less likely to do so. The oldest Lutheran church in North America, in New York City, established a Lutheran school in 1752. In 2007-2008 (National Center for Educational Statistics) the Lutheran Church–Missouri Synod (LCMS) had 1,200 schools with 138,000 students, the Wisconsin Evangelical Lutheran Synod (WELS) had 344 schools with 30,000 students, and the Evangelical Lutheran Church in America (ELCA) had 180 schools with 14,000 students. Although it is somewhat of a generalization, LCMS and the WELS grew out of the German immigration and the ELCA grew out of the Scandinavian immigration. Although WELS and LCMS have less than half the membership of the ELCA, they have the great majority of elementary and secondary schools.

As Norman Madson noted in an anniversary booklet, both the Scandinavians and the Germans emigrated from countries in which the state provided a Lutheran education. When they came to the U.S., they were confronted with a public school which did not include religious instruction and where the teaching was in English. The Norwegians, Swedes, and Danes had less difficulty accepting public education at the elementary level and were less insistent on preserving their mother tongue. They also tended to come with skills and occupations which required a quick assimilation into the existing culture, including language and associations. Georg Sverdrup (1848-1907), a Norwegian theologian, also contended that the state, not the church, was responsible for education, and churches should not use their money to do the work of the state. The Scandinavians thus tended to establish colleges which would provide Christian training for young people, both to move into the American society and to be Christian teachers in public schools. That became the basis for the great Lutheran colleges in the Midwest.

The Germans, on the other hand, for complex reasons wanted to preserve the language that Luther used and they wanted to raise their children in a German culture. The early theologians of the LCMS, WELS, and, later, the Evangelical Lutheran Synod (ELS), such as Walther, Hoenecke, and Madson believed that Lutheran schools were essential, not merely for language and cultural preservation, but also that the Bible could be read and studied and taught by teachers who were trained by the Lutheran church for Lutheran elementary schools. The battles at the beginning of the twentieth century over the Bennett Law and in legal attempts to restrict or close parochial schools strengthened the resolve of the WELS, LCMS, and ELS to preserve their schools so the next generation could also contend for the faith. The LCMS, WELS, and ELS thus established colleges to train teachers for their own schools.

From the 1920s onward, culture and language became less relevant as a reason for Lutheran parochial schools, and Lutheran schools

Zion Lutheran Parochial School, Hampton, Nebraska, in 1920.

became "Americanized." Public schools became more professional and had access to financial resources that private schools did not. The boom years after World War II dramatically increased the enrollments in Lutheran schools. Today, Lutheran schools face declining enrollments which mirror declines in birth rates and in the number of church-going Lutherans. Schools also face the expense of maintaining buildings, keeping current with technology, and meeting the new emphasis on effectiveness and accountability. Other non-public schools, such as the Catholics, face similar challenges. On the positive side, there is a growing interest in early childhood education which goes across all the Lutheran church bodies. Early childhood education has become important in evangelism and in meeting a need for today's families. Today, eleven percent of all children in pre-kindergarten through grade twelve in the United States attend a nonpublic school. Schools such as Lutheran schools provide a necessary choice for parents, and they provide a means by which a church can assist parents in the most important part of a child's education.

Numbers and statistics, however, cannot encompass or fully explain what a Lutheran school did in the past or does today. For that you really need a story:

> It was a warm March day. Winter was over—maybe. The two classrooms in the Lutheran school were filled with children, quiet and busy. In the upper grade room the teacher was reading *Evangeline* to the students. The girls would cry when Gabriel died; the boys toughed it out. Across the playground, the church bells rang. Then the middle bell began tolling. 1, 2, 3—someone had died—79, 80, 81. Someone really old had died. Toward the end of the school day, the pastor handed the teacher/organist the hymn numbers and the hymn the family wanted the children to sing—"Asleep in Jesus"—again. On the day of the funeral, the boys brought along slacks, dress shirt, and a tie. The girls wore their dresses. Before the funeral at 2:00 (only Catholics had funerals in the morning), the boys changed and the upper grades were marched over to church, down the center aisle, around the open coffin, and upstairs to the balcony. The teacher/organist/sexton played, the pastor preached, and the children sang. When

all the people left the church for the cemetery, the children were marched back to school, quietly. No recess was scheduled in the afternoon because friends and family returned to the church for the *Leichenschmous*. But at the end of the school day, the ladies aid brought the left-over cake from the funeral meal for the children. It was a good day. Several weeks later, the teacher/organist/sexton/principal announced that the school had received a memorial gift from the family, and the children should decide where it would be spent. The children decided on an unabridged dictionary—the boys lost out on the baseball and bat because the girls sided with the teacher/organist/sexton/principal/janitor who had the last word anyway. A month later the dictionary arrived and was neatly inscribed: *A gift of the Volksmanner family in memory of Gertrude Elizabeth Anna Volksmanner (1860-1941)*. The dictionary would be used by her great-great-grandson when he enrolled the following year. First grader Mary Ann Leitner also announced that she had a new baby sister.

Life, death, and continuity—those were the lessons taught by the community of Lutheran church and Lutheran school to each generation. Perhaps it was insular, perhaps parochial. But the school and the church remain with those children.

BILL SCHAEFFER

American Lutherans and the Civil War

The American Civil War (1861-1865), a bloody and destructive conflict, represents a crucial turning point in American history and one that affected all aspects of our society. American Lutherans were profoundly influenced by the war, and in some sections of the country Lutheranism was severely affected by its events. Sorrow and suffering were strangers to few homes during this time, and the nation mourned even as it fought.

Though many other issues may have contributed to the war, the chief dispute was slavery, especially its expansion into the new western territories. Though few Lutherans in the North were radical abolitionists (the Franckean Synod being an exception), most northern Lutherans tended to oppose slavery and its extension. Most southern Lutherans had eventually come to support the system of slavery, and the question of slavery had complicated their relations with their northern counterparts. While some American Lutherans supported the mediating policy of the Democrats, increasingly the northern Lutherans (especially the new immigrants) were drawn to the newly organized Republican party.

With the election of Lincoln in 1860, the long-simmering national tensions erupted into divisions and conflict, as the southern states withdrew from the Union and formed the Confederate States of America. Following many other southern religious groups, southern Lutherans withdrew from their northern counterparts and in 1863 formed a new organization, eventually known as the General Synod, South. Lutherans in border states, such as Missouri and Tennessee, watched cautiously as the conflict erupted into warfare in the spring of 1861. It would be the southern Lutherans (mainly in Virginia, North Carolina, and South Carolina) and Lutherans in the border states who would bear the direct effects of the war that stretched out for the next four years.

On both sides of the conflicts, American Lutherans rushed to support their governments, and many Lutherans enlisted in their respective armies. There were numbers of regiments in the Union army made up of young German and Scandinavian immigrants, often Lutherans, and Lutheran pastors volunteered to accompany these regiments as chaplains (notably Claus Clausen, William Passavant, and John H. W. Stuckenberg). Various Lutheran groups, North and South, organized to support their soldiers in the field, sending supplies and religious materials to the armies when possible. Support for the two respective governments was strong though some Lutherans, worried about possible transgression of the line separating church and state, and held back.

Claus Clausen

John H. W. Stuckenberg

The war came home directly to northern Lutherans in the summer of 1863, when Con-

Schmucker Hall (above) was the seminary's main classroom and dormitory during the time of the Civil War battle at Gettysburg. Both Union and Confederate armies used the cupola as an observation spot. The building became a hospital later in the battle.

An artillery shell remains embedded in the Schmucker Hall wall (right).

federate troops pushed into southern Pennsylvania and fought a climatic battle with Union forces at the little town of Gettysburg. This town just also happened to contain the oldest Lutheran seminary in the United States, and much of the battle turned upon the possession of the Seminary Ridge, the geographical feature on which the Lutheran seminary itself stood. The destruction of the battle itself caused a great deal of damage to the Gettysburg seminary, and the students and faculty were displaced for an extended period of time. Tensions in Missouri in the early months of the war also threatened Concordia Seminary in St. Louis, and students there briefly formed a company to defend the campus.

But it was in the South, especially in Virginia and the Carolinas, where Lutherans were most directly affected, especially in 1864 and 1865, as Union troops pushed into the South. By this time the war had become a bloody, destructive conflict from which civilian property and institutions were not exempt. Already the northern blockade and the demands of war had seriously impoverished many southern Lutherans, but direct warfare added further miseries, especially during Sherman's march to the sea. Some Lutheran congregations were damaged or destroyed by the war and its effects. Southern Lutheran institutions, such as Roanoke College, Newberry College, and Southern Seminary, collapsed from lack of students and funding. The armies of both sides confiscated properties and goods for use in the war effort, and few places were left unscathed.

With the end of this war in April 1865, the direct conflicts ceased, though the effects of war would continue to be sharp for many years, especially in the South. The eastern Lutherans would continue to be divided North and South for the next fifty years; they would eventually come to be formally reunited in 1918.

MARK GRANQUIST

Lutherans in Madagascar

If you were asked to list some of the largest and fastest growing Lutheran churches in the world, you would probably not think first of the Malagasy Lutheran Church on the African island of Madagascar. But to the surprise of many, the Malagasy Lutheran Church is, at three million members, the third largest Lutheran church in Africa (only the Lutheran churches in Ethiopia and Tanzania have more members) and one of the fastest growing Lutheran churches in the world.

Madagascar as a country is located on an island east of the southern tip of Africa. In many ways its isolation from that continent has meant that it is a country of unique plants and animals, and a very distinctive human culture, with influences from Indonesia and Africa, as well as Arab traders. The Kingdom of Madagascar was taken over as a French colony in 1895 and became an independent country again in 1960. Roman Catholic missionaries began work on the island as early as the sixteenth century, and Protestant missions were begun in the nineteenth century. Today the Malagasy people are about equally divided between those who practice traditional religious and those who are Christians (Protestants and Roman Catholics are about even). Many Malagasy people combine traditional beliefs and practices with Christianity.

Lutheran missionaries from Norway began to arrive in the country in 1866, and began their work at the southern part of the country. Their mission was greatly assisted by two factors: the conversion of the royal court to Christianity in 1869, and the translation of the Bible and other

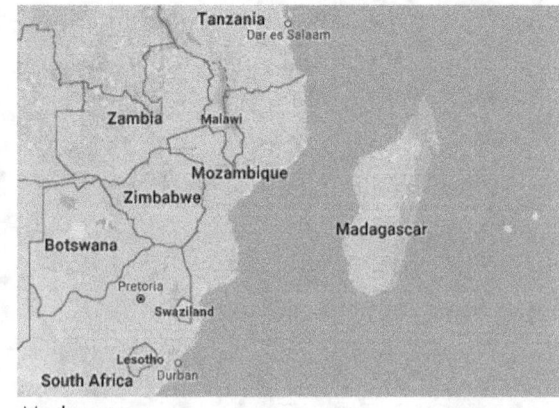
Madagascar

materials into the Malagasy language. In 1888 Norwegian-American missionaries arrived in the country and began to work in the southwestern part of the island, beginning an American Lutheran presence on the island that still continues. Protestant mission efforts were at a disadvantage to the Roman Catholics during the French colonial period, but the Lutheran mission churches grew steadily, along with medical and educational outreach. The two missions cooperated, and in 1950 their 1,800 congregations were united in the newly-formed Malagasy Lutheran Church (in Malagasy, Fiangonana Loterana Malagasy or FLM), which became a part of the Lutheran World Federation. The first Lutheran seminary on the island was established in 1871 in Fiananarntsoa, and Malagasy Lutherans have been educated as pastors, teachers, and catechists there and at other schools of the church. The first Malagasy pastor to head the church was elected in 1961, a year after the country's independence.

An early missionary to Madagascar with indigenous children

The Malagasy Lutheran church has grown rapidly since independence, with membership increasing from about 840,000 in 1988 to three million today. The FLM has a large number of catechists, especially in the rural areas, and seeks to expand from its base in the southern and central parts of the island into the northern parts, where Christianity is much less strong. As with many other churches in Africa, the Malagasy Lutheran Church is strongly positioned with a network of schools and educational institutions across the island. It also runs an important system of social service agencies (hospitals, clinics, and care facilities) as well as development projects to better the lives of the Malagasy people (in cooperation with its mission partners in the Lutheran World Federation). The FLM is an important part of the fabric of this country, which now numbers over twenty-two million people.

One of the distinct feature of Christianity in Madagascar is a deeply rooted tradition of healing and exorcism among the people in what is known as the Fifohazana movement. This indigenous revival movement began in 1894 with a vision seen by a man named Rainisoalambo, who was an aristocrat and traditional healer in the southern part of the island. Rainisoalambo was told to put away his traditional idols and become a Christian. He initiated an awakening movement that has permeated many areas of Malagasy Christian life, including the FLM. This movement concentrates on spiritual healing, exorcisms, service to the poor, Bible study, and fervent witnessing to others. In the Fifohazana community centers, people are trained to become "shepherds" (*mpiandry*) who take care of the sick and handicapped in their communities. Others, called "apostles" are trained to take the gospel message into areas of the country where Christianity is not well established. This strong spiritual emphasis is important for the health of the Malagasy Lutheran Church and its recent growth. Many of its church leaders have come out of the Fifohazana movement. There are times where this movement has come into conflict with more traditional Christian church systems, but Christian leaders work to ensure that they cooperate together for the good of the Christian movement in the country.

The Malagasy Republic is one of the poorest countries on the planet and faces many challenges. Yet the Christians in the country, including Malagasy Lutherans, are working to support the people of the country and the growth of the Christian message among them.

MARK GRANQUIST

Theological Fights: The Question of Predestination

In traveling around the small towns and rural areas of the Upper Midwest, it is common to encounter areas where there are a number of different, small Lutheran churches right in the same local area, sometimes within blocks of each other. Sometimes the existence of these "neighborly" congregations can be traced to ethnic or linguistic origins; in many towns there are "Swedish" or "Norwegian" or "Danish" or "German" or "Finnish" churches. But in a number of these "clustered" situations, the existence of multiple congregations in close proximity can be traced back to theological arguments that raged among Midwestern Lutherans during the latter part of the nineteenth century. Sometimes these theological debates got so intense that they split congregations, resulting in two or more congregations where there had been only one.

The theological fight in question raged during the 1870s and 1880s over the question of predestination (or election). First, something about predestination and then about the fight among the Lutherans.

Predestination is the idea that God has selected (or predetermined) ahead of time those who will be saved. This is a doctrine that is most often associated with Reformed (Calvinist) Christians, but it is an important for many Christians, especially Lutherans. Predestina-

> We know that all things work together for good* for those who love God, who are called according to his purpose. For those whom he foreknew he also predestined to be conformed to the image of his Son, in order that he might be the firstborn within a large family. And those whom he predestined he also called; and those whom he called he also justified; and those whom he justified he also glorified.
>
> ROMANS 8:28-30

tion is important because it defends the idea of grace and stresses that people are saved solely by God's grace, and not by their works. However, predestination is a problem to some people who do not like the idea; it seems to some to be unworthy of a loving God or it may seem to negate the need for human moral action. If your salvation is pre-determined, why should you bother to be good? But then, if human moral action "counts," does that not negate the grace of God? It is a complicated and perennial theological debate. The Lutheran confessional document of the sixteenth century (that officially defined Lutheran theology) affirms predestination but does not fully define it, and Lutherans have continued to wrestle with those questions.

Beginning in 1877, this question flared up among German and Norwegian Lutherans in the Midwest. The dispute involved different German groups, the Missouri Synod in opposition to the Ohio and Iowa Synods, and then later among Norwegian Lutherans. An American Lutheran historian has explained it this way:

> The man who believes in Christ and his atoning merit is . . . predestined to be saved. But shall we say that God's predestination is the cause of his faith and his salvation, or shall we say that his faith is the cause of his predestination? The Missourians took the first alternative . . . [insisting] that a man cannot believe in Christ unless God causes him to do so. . . . [Missouri's opponents] took the second alternative and insisted that God elects man to salvation "in view of his faith" in the merits of Christ.[1]

To its opponents, the Missouri Synod's position sounded like fatalism and, even worse, like the position of the Calvinists (an irony, because the founders of Missouri were staunch opponents of Calvinist theology). The position of the Ohio and Iowa Synods, that God foresees (foreknowledge) peoples' faith and grants salvation on that basis, seemed to the Missourians to be dangerously close to "works righteousness" or the idea that humans can earn their own salvation. This battle raged in among German-American Lutherans for at least a dozen years and caused a long-running rift between these synods.

---

[1] Abdel Ross Wentz, *A Basic History of Lutheranism in America*, revised edition (Philadelphia: Fortress Press, 1964), 206.

Among Norwegian-American Lutherans, this fight divided the Norwegian Synod and caused quite a few congregations to split over the issue. The main part of the Norwegian Synod sided with the Missouri position, but a significant minority opposed it. In 1884 this minority group formed the "Anti-Missouri Brotherhood" and split from the Norwegian Synod, to join with other Norwegian Lutheran denominations in 1890 to form the United Norwegian Lutheran Church. This battle split congregations as well; in one instance, at the East Koshkonong parish outside of Madison, Wisconsin, the dissidents broke away and built a new Lutheran church literally just across the parking lot from the older congregation.

To some, all this fighting might seem ridiculous, or worse; why should Christians fight like this among themselves? And certainly church fights can, at times, be caused in part by human, sinful factors, which is wrong. But remember that theology does matter, and these Lutherans were taking theological matters seriously. Trying to understand God, and to make sure that salvation is by God's grace alone, is extremely important—important enough, at times, to fight over (within the bounds of Christian love). Sometimes a struggle can result in a clearer, stronger Christian faith.

MARK GRANQUIST

Germans from Russia in U.S. Lutheranism

Catherine II the Great, czarina of Russia, began life in Germany (1729) as a Prussian princess. In 1745 she married the designated heir to the Russian throne, Peter, and was baptized into the Russian Orthodox Church. Peter became Czar Peter III in early 1762 but abdicated six months later, and Catherine assumed the Imperial throne. She had ambitious plans for Russia and initiated immediate reforms, promoting education, improving trade, and inviting immigrants who had farming skills to settle on open land in Russia's south. In 1762 she issued an edict inviting people (except Jews) from all the countries of Europe to settle in the lower Volga frontier. The first edict lured few immigrants, but a second one in 1763 offered specific benefits: Keep your language and cultural/religious tradition, pay no taxes, govern your communities without Russian control, do no military service, and own land in perpetuity.

Catherine the Great

The first group of German immigrants reached their Volga destination in 1764, and by 1798 there were more than 38,000 Germans in Russia. Later large numbers of Germans settled in the Odessa region north of the Black Sea. These colonists formed communities largely on specific religious affiliation: Lutheran, Mennonite, Reformed, or Roman Catholic. All told, 1.7 million Germans, seventy-three percent of them Lutherans, settled in Russia mostly along the Volga River and north of the Black Sea. When Catherine died in 1796, Alexander I renewed her pledges in 1804 and 1813. But there was a growing antagonism to the privileges given the German settlers spread across the empire, who were seen as an economic and political threat. The freedoms promised by Catherine were systematically removed, and by 1871 a decree repealed the privileges the colonists enjoyed for over a century.

These actions were seen as an unconscionable breach

The main street in Balzar, a German town in Russia, with the Lutheran church on the right

of faith by the German colonists. Many of them had a tradition of anti-militarism, and they were particularly distressed when a six-year military service law came into force. The new military conscription unleashed the first large wave of emigration of Germans from Russia, chiefly to America. To this day, photos of young Germans in Russian military uniforms found in American homes of their descendants reveal that some families were forced to yield to the Russian draft before emigrating.

The Homestead Act, adopted in 1862, was designed to open the U.S. Midwest for extensive settlement. Many immigrant Germans from Russia took advantage of this offer and began life in their new country on 160 acres of farmland, typically in territories of the Great Plains—Kansas, Colorado, Nebraska, and the Dakotas. The German exodus from Russia began in the early 1870s when about forty families settled in the vicinity of Yankton, South Dakota.

As they had in Russia, the Germans coming to America usually filled new communities here with people of the same faith identity. One of the first things Lutheran Germans from Russia did when settling in their new community was to build a church, usually from the memory of their church back in the homeland. The German language was dominant in congregations until suspicions created by World War I pressured many to switch entirely to English. Yet, in some communities the use of German in church continued as late as World War II.

Differing church customs and traditions at times made harmony in one united congregation difficult. Lutheran congregations of

Germans from Russia were known to split over doctrinal issues and affiliate with different branches of Lutheranism. Early congregations joined the General Synod, the Ohio Synod, or, in the Dakotas, the Iowa Synod, which helped form the 1930 American Lutheran Church. The Lutheran Church–Missouri Synod and Wisconsin Evangelical Lutheran Synod also gained congregations of German Lutherans from Russia.

The Great Depression of the 1930s caused immeasurable problems for many of the Lutheran Germans from Russia. The terrible dust storms during this time caused widespread crop failure year after year. Large groups of Russian Germans from the Dakotas, Nebraska, Kansas, and Colorado moved to Washington, California, and Texas. Others who survived the Depression and the dust storms became prosperous where they were located. They preserved their ethnic identity undergirded by a staunch faith in God, worked very hard, determined to create a decent livelihood from the good earth. Their farming practices became more mechanized. Rural electrification transformed their lives. The rural one-room school house was replaced by consolidated schools to which farm children were bussed. Some of their children who grew up on prairie farms left their homes and moved to larger towns and cities.

As older generations of Germans from Russia have passed on, an entire folk culture is disappearing, leaving only a memory among their descendants. However, the influence from the Lutheran Germans from Russia in the U.S. are deeply woven into the warp and woof of America's fabric, especially among Lutherans.

WILLIS S. GERTNER

Forgotten Giant: Johan Arndt Aasgaard

The mystery: There's no history. The first item on the agenda, when Johan Arndt Aasgaard's biography finally is written, is why no one has written the life of one who led practically all Norwegian Lutherans in the United States for twenty-nine years. There is no obvious reason. Aasgaard was a kind of Lutheran Horatio Alger Jr., rising from poverty to prominence. When that biography is written, the author will take up at least four major themes.

Pastor, in all that he did. That he had a pastoral heart is illustrated by an oft-told family story: "A woman came into Granper's office for confession. She had had an affair and was devastated. She confessed all to her pastor, wept, and prayed. Pastor Aasgaard gave his confessor absolution. When she was leaving, she asked: "Pastor Aasgaard, what do I do now?" "Do, my child? About what?" "About my sin, Pastor." To which her pastor replied: "What sin?" Although his name echoes Johann Arndt, the famous seventeenth century pietist, Aasgaard belonged to the United Lutherans, the conservative but centrist branch of Norwegian Lutherans, which incorporated elements of both Haugean pietism and the strict confessionalism of the Norwegian Synod. He was pastor full time at Norway Grove, De Forest, Wisconsin, from 1901-1911, and part time at Salem, Salem, North Dakota, during his years as president of Concordia College.

Johan Arndt Aasgaard

Leader, spectacular but not flamboyant. Aasgaard is remembered as outspoken, yet at the same time one who was tactful and gentle. These qualities stood him in good stead as he raised money, first of all in his parish, then for Concordia College (1911-1925), as president (1925-1954) for the colleges of the Norwegian Lutheran Church of America during and after the Great Depression of the 1930s, and for relief work in Europe during and after World War II. These qualities also stood him in good stead as he helped three differing groups of Norwegian Lutherans grow into one church, helped immigrants and the next generation become Americans, and prepared the way for larger American Lutheran unity and Christian unity that took place soon after he retired. Aasgaard always was a hard worker, yet he also rose to prominence because he was recognized as a natural leader, one who could be trusted to point the way forward.

Educator, in small and in large. Already in the parish Aasgaard stressed the importance of Sunday school and confirmation for children: "They will have, like the Prodigal Son, something that is essential if they are going to not only stay in their baptismal covenant, but even return if they wander away." He had done further study at Princeton Theological Seminary and the University of Wisconsin, which led to teaching church history at the United Seminary, St. Paul, Minnesota, in 1906-1907. He edited the *United Lutheran* from 1908-1909 and the *Kirkebladet* from 1910-1911. Immediately, when he decided in 1911 to leave his parish in Wisconsin, Concordia College in Moorhead invited him to become president, and he established a solid future for the college both by fundraising and by raising academic standards.

Johan Arndt Aasgaard

Citizen, of the United States and of the world. Unexpectedly, in 1925, Aasgaard became president of the Norwegian Lutheran Church of America. At his retirement in 1954, when asked what had been his greatest professional accomplishment, he stated, "I delivered the Norwegian Lutherans safely to the American shore"—which he had, though at times leading Norwegian Lutherans must have seemed like trying to herd cats. Again, his tact and gentleness, his obvious sense of the way forward, stood him in good stead. He was committed to helping immigrant Lutherans take on the American way of life: the separation of church and state, freedom of conscience, the democratic process. Much of his energy was spent on "home missions," starting and shepherding congregations as well as charitable institutions. Yet Norwegians have also had a strong commitment to global missions, and, because of the Norwegian merger in 1917 and the disaster of World War II, Aasgaard was necessarily involved in promoting missions around the world. Again because of the disaster of World War II, along with other Lutheran leaders in the United States, he raised millions to provide relief for Lutherans in Europe and especially in his case for Norway. His personal friendship with one of the heroes of the Norwegian resistance, Bishop Eivind Berggrav of Oslo, is part of the saga.

As O. G. Malmin wrote in the *Lutheran Herald* at the time of JAA's funeral: He was "God's man for a particular time in a particular place. He fulfilled his ministry with devotion and dedication."

MEG MADSON

Preachers, Pietists, and Socialists: Finns in North America

"The Finns are different." This sentiment, by a Finnish-American leader, expresses a reality that sometimes is not always acknowledged—that the experiences of Finnish immigrants to North America differ in significant ways from those of other Lutherans. Finnish immigrants are often lumped together with those from Sweden, Norway, and Denmark, and usually as an afterthought. But this is to miss the distinctive factors behind the Finnish immigration.

To start with, Finland in the nineteenth century was a subject nation. For a long period of its history it was ruled and influenced by Sweden, although after 1809 it was taken from Sweden and given to the Russian Empire. As with many other European peoples, there was a strong birth of Finnish nationalism in the late nineteenth century, especially in reaction to Russian domination. A number of Finnish immigrants left Finland so that their sons would not be conscripted into the Russian Imperial army. This burning new nationalism was translated into a Finnish pride and independence among immigrants to North America.

As well, the Finnish immigrants came later than other Lutherans; Finnish immigration did not begin in earnest until the 1880s and 1890s. By this time the American frontier was closed, and most of the good agricultural land was already taken. Finnish immigrants found jobs in mining, timbering, fishing, and in factories in the Midwest and Pacific Northwest U.S. and in Canada. Even today the northern areas of Michigan (the Upper Peninsula), Wisconsin, and Minnesota (the Iron Range) are the traditional heartland of Finnish-Americans, with significant Finnish colonies elsewhere.

The economic and geographic settlements of the Finns in North America meant that they were located differently from many other Lutherans, who were essentially agricultural. The mining, timbering, and factory sections of the economy at this time were at the center of the new labor movements, both in Finland and North America.

These movements were often socialist in orientation and viewed the leaders of the Christian churches as being unconcerned with the vocational and personal concerns of working people. There was a strong Finnish element in the labor and socialist (and even communist) movements in the nineteenth and twentieth centuries in North America.

There were, however, also strong religious awakenings in nineteenth century Finland, and many immigrants brought with them a deep grounding in the Lutheranism of the Church of Finland, as well as a burning religiosity from the Pietist and awakening movements. Finland was overwhelmingly Lutheran, and revival leaders such as Paavo Ruotsalainen, Frederik Hedberg, and Lars Levi Laestadius preached fiery awakenings that strengthened the people's faith as well as challenged the official Church of Finland. This religiosity also set up conflicts between the official church (the Preachers), the newly-awakened (the Pietists), and those cool toward religion (the Socialists), which rolled through the immigrant communities.

Paavo Ruotsalainen

Frederik Hedberg

Finnish-American Lutheranism took on several different organizational forms in North America. Although the first Finnish Lutheran congregation in North America was formed in 1876, the formation of such congregations was slow, especially due to a severe shortage of pastors as well as serious economic challenges. It was not until 1890 that these initial congregations were drawn together into a denominational structure, the Finnish Evangelical Lutheran Church, popularly known as the Suomi Synod. This group became the largest religious group among Finns in North America; of all the religious groups, it was probably closest to the Church of Finland, although it also had deep roots in the Finnish awakenings, especially those of Ruotsalainen. This denomination opened a seminary and school at Hancock, Michigan, which is now Finlandia University.

Not all Finnish Lutherans joined the Suomi Synod. Another group of Finnish Lutherans, mainly inspired by the awakening led by Frederik Hedberg, in 1898 formed a second, smaller group, the Finnish Evangelical Lutheran National Church in America (the "National" Finns). This second denomination came under the influence of the Lutheran Church–Missouri Synod in the 1920s and eventually became a part of the LCMS in 1964. A third group of Finnish Lutherans were those who followed revival leader Lars Levi Laestadius, known as the Apostolic or Laestadian Lutherans, which is a uniquely Finnish form of Christianity, emphasizing emotional preaching for conversion and repentance, and individual laying-on of hands and absolution. This movement, both in Finland and North America, has been led by charismatic individuals but has had a history of schism and divisions. In North America they are divided into at least twenty different groups, some much like other conservative evangelical Christians and some strictly removed from "the world."

Lars Levi Laestadius

Since the Finnish immigrants arrived later than many others and tended to be isolated, many congregations maintained at least some worship in Finnish well into the twentieth century.

MARK GRANQUIST

The Lutheran Fraternal Phenomenon

A non-Lutheran mainline Christian was heard to declare, "I sure wish our denomination had a deal going like the Lutherans have." When pressed, she explained: "Those fraternal groups [North American Lutherans had two at the time] do amazing things for the church. Why didn't our church think of something like that?"

Members of our Lutheran congregations may be tempted to conclude that Thrivent Financial for Lutherans and its predecessors, Aid Association for Lutherans and Lutheran Brotherhood, were insurance companies created

to corner a captive market (Lutherans). They'd be mistaken.

Lutherans haven't always had "mutual aid" societies. And when they created them, the idea wasn't so much to milk the Lutheran market with insurance sales, but rather to help Lutherans look out for one another. In fact, the original names adopted by these societies give no hint they were insurance companies at all.

The Iowa Synod (which later became part of the "old" American Lutheran Church) seems to have gone first. In 1879 convention delegates, sitting in the pews of St. John Lutheran Church, Maxfield Township (rural Denver, ten miles from Waverly) organized *Unterstuetzungs Verein*. Needless to say, the vote was taken in German. Later renamed Lutheran Mutual Aid Society, the company moved to Waverly, down the street from Wartburg College. Never a fraternal, the society survived for 105 years before giving up its Lutheran identity. (Today it's a firm providing insurance for members of credit unions.)

Two other attempts at providing "mutual aid" for Lutherans both became fraternals. (For more about what a "fraternal" is and does, keep reading.) Aid Association for Lutherans (AAL) was one of these. It was created within the Lutheran Synodical Conference (no longer in existence) in Appleton, Wisconsin, in 1902. For nearly a century, the Aid Association (note the lack of "insurance" in the title) served German Lutherans, a large swath of whom belonged to the Lutheran Church–Missouri Synod. One of the selling points for founding AAL was that, at the time, working class Lutherans couldn't find affordable insurance. AAL helped solve that problem.

Lutheran Brotherhood (LB) arrived next on the scene. Like AAL, LB was created as a fraternal, to provide mutual support in this case for Norwegian Lutherans. Like Lutheran Mutual, it was created by vote of delegates at a church convention. But the 1917 Minneapolis meeting that birthed it was contentious. Some delegates thought insurance might not be pleasing to God. (Perhaps it suggested to them a lack of trust in the Almighty during tough times.) So the proponents described it as a "mutual aid society" and named it "Luther Union." The Union merged with the Lutheran Brotherhood of America in 1920. The latter group's name was adopted.

After a century of fierce competition, AAL and LB quietly merged in 2001. Under the new name, Thrivent, North American Lutherans found themselves with the largest fraternal benefit society in the U.S.

So, what's a "fraternal benefit society," and why do Lutherans like having one of them? (Pardon the sexist language: "Fraternal" is a male term, but women are very much invested in this enterprise—even though there was a time when AAL's male membership had to take a vote that finally allowed women to own policies!)

A fraternal benefit society enjoys special treatment under tax law. It's considered a non-profit organization, functioning for the benefit of its members. In the case of AAL, LB and (now) Thrivent, the members are the owners of company shares (or certificates or insurance policies). But, in a broader sense, the members are all of us Lutherans. So, whether you own a financial stake in Thrivent or not, you as a Lutheran are a beneficiary.

How does that work? Under its charter, the fraternal provides financial support to its members. The Lutheran fraternals have historically done it in several ways. Lutheran groups (usually working through one of the fraternal's local branches) can launch a charitable project and receive matching funds from the fraternal. The project could be as local as helping a family pay its medical bills or a sponsoring fund-raiser to stock a food shelf. It could be as far-reaching as helping raise money for a Habitat for Humanity house or for Haiti earthquake relief.

Lutheran denominations have received thousands of dollars in fraternal support over the years. That means that many churchwide programs developed by ELCA, LCMS, WELS, or any other Lutheran judicatory can be—and have been through the years—underwritten with support from the fraternal society. Similar support has flowed over the years to Lutheran colleges, universities, seminaries, Bible camps, and a host of other Lutheran institutions.

MICHAEL L. SHERER

Lutherans in Papua New Guinea

Lutherans literally can be found all around the world, in every kind of culture and ethnic setting. Perhaps the most distinctive Lutheran success story can be found in the southeast Asian country of Papua New Guinea, where Christians now number ninety-five percent of the entire country, and Lutherans comprise almost twenty percent of that population. This in a place where Christianity was unknown until 130 years ago, and whose terrain and settlement patterns have made Christian expansion very difficult.

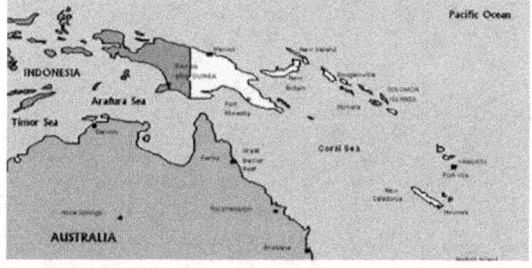

The country of Papua New Guinea occupies the eastern half of the large island of New Guinea, just north of Australia. (The eastern half is the Indonesian province of Papua.) It is an island of very rough and mountainous terrain, and even today over eighty percent its people live in tribal villages in isolated rural areas, often quite independent of each other. This is a country of 850 different languages and over a thousand different cultural groups, where many people live traditional lifestyles. Although European explorers encountered this region in the sixteenth century, western colonialism only came to the island in 1884, when the island was divided between Holland (west), Germany (northeast), and Britain (southeast). Even then, colonial administration touched only the coastal regions of the island.

Johannes Flierl

German missionaries from the Neuendettlsau and Rhenish mission societies began work in the German territory in 1886 with pioneering pastor Johannes Flierl, who worked in New Guinea from 1886 to 1930; he was soon joined by other colleagues from Germany. Though these missionaries made limited progress, the terrain and culture made it difficult at first for them to

Johannes Flierl with the people he served in Papua New Guinea

extend their work into the rural areas. In 1908 the first New Guinean evangelists were sent out, beginning a long pattern of indigenous leadership. Given the geographical situation, they adopted a successful pattern of evangelism that focused on the conversion of entire villages and tribal units, so that Christian converts would not be isolated from their families and tribes. Evangelists postponed the baptism of individual new converts until the entire social unit was ready to adopt Christianity. Local New Guinean congregations were encouraged to send out Christian workers to bring the Christian message to other local communities. Slowly the Lutheran missions began to move into the highland rural areas, but conditions there were very difficult, especially for Western missionaries. Portions of the Bible were translated into the larger local languages.

As a part of the First World War, Australian troops took over the German territory in 1914; German missionaries were removed, and not allowed to return until 1927. American Lutheran missionaries from the Iowa Synod came to New Guinea to fill the void left by the expulsion of the German missionaries, and those Americans remained on the island through the twentieth century. Lutheran missionaries also came from the Lutheran church in Australia because of British and Australian administration of the region. Another disruption occurred during the Second World War, but American and

German missionaries were able to return after 1945. Missionaries from the Lutheran Church–Missouri Synod began work in the Enga region in 1948, and there was a successful post-war expansion of Lutheranism on the island.

The post-war era saw the expansion of Lutheran educational institutions on the island, especially schools to train pastors and evangelists, and other programs for social workers, teachers, and lay parish assistants. Although there were Bible translations into a number of different local languages, the linguistic challenges of work in so many different languages was immense. During and after the Second World War a new common language, Neo-Melanesian (commonly known as Pidgin) gained widespread acceptance; though much of the church education is in English, this new language remains important, and the Bible has been translated into it.

The Lutheran Mission in New Guinea (LMNG) was formed in 1953 to coordinate the Western missionary work on the island, and in 1956 the Evangelical Lutheran Church in New Guinea was formed (at independence the word "Papua" was added). The Missouri Synod mission formed the Gutnuis (Good News) Lutheran Church in 1961. With the country's independence in 1975 both churches became autonomous, and both are now independent members of the Lutheran World Federation.

As with many newly-independent countries, Papua New Guinea faces challenging social and economic problems, especially since the twentieth-century intrusion of Western culture is such a clash with traditional Papua New Guinean society. The Lutheran churches continue to receive grants from the LWF for religious and development work, and some Western personnel continue to assist these churches. Currently, the population of Papua New Guinea is about seven million people, with about ninety-five percent Christian. The Evangelical Lutheran Church in Papua New Guinea has about 1.2 million members, while the Gutnuis Lutheran Church-Papua New Guinea has 150,000 members. Quite an accomplishment for 130 years! With God anything is possible!

MARK GRANQUIST

Icelandic Lutherans in North America

Although they were never a sizable part of the Lutheran community in North America, Icelandic Lutherans nevertheless formed their own distinctive portion of it. Mainly centered in the areas of northeastern North Dakota and southern Manitoba, Icelandic Lutherans formed their own synod in 1885, which remained independent until uniting with a larger denomination in 1940. Congregations with Icelandic roots today are generally associated either with the Evangelical Lutheran Church in America or the Evangelical Lutheran Church in Canada.

A small island in the North Atlantic between Norway and Greenland, Iceland has been Lutheran since the Reformation. Icelandic immigration to North America between 1870 and 1900 is estimated at about 15,000 people, out of a total population of only 70,000. Though their main settlements were in and around the colony of New Iceland (near Winnipeg, Manitoba), other groups formed scattered communities, especially in the Puget Sound region of Washington.

The first Icelandic settlers struggled to establish local Lutheran congregations in North America, led by two Icelandic pastors, Pall (Paul) Thorlaksson and Jon Bjarnason. Thorlaksson was a part of the Norwegian Synod, educated at Concordia Seminary in St. Louis, while Bjarnason was educated in Iceland. Eventually in 1885, Bjarnason, along with a newly ordained pastor Hans Thorgrimsen, organized the Icelandic Evangelical Lutheran Synod of America, with a total of twelve congregations. This Synod remained independent for the next fifty-five years, though because of its

Jon Bjarnason

Pall Thorlaksson

small size it had to rely on larger Lutheran groups (usually Norwegian) for ministerial training and other assistance. When, in 1940, the synod voted to become a separate ethnic synod within the larger United Lutheran Church in America (ULCA), it consisted of fifteen pastors, forty-six congregations, and 6,760 baptized members. In 1962, when the ULCA merged with other Lutheran groups to form the Lutheran Church in America (LCA), the separate Icelandic Synod was disbanded.

Icelanders have a general reputation for being tough, independent-minded, and sometimes stubborn people, perhaps coming from their centuries-long struggle to survive on a barren, wind-swept island in the North Atlantic. Those who came to North America have generally shown these traits; one Icelandic-American writer bemoaned the fact that his people walked over hundreds of miles of rich farming territory in the Midwest, settling instead in a sandy-soiled region that reminded them of home. Iceland has strong democratic institutions and traditions going back to the tenth century, with equally strong traditional rights for women. The Icelandic Synod was noteworthy for being the first Lutheran denomination in North America to allow women to vote and hold congregational offices and to be voting delegates to synodical meetings. Lay people took control in the synod, far outnumbering clergy delegates at synodical meetings.

These traditions worked to keep the synod independent as long as it could, but often resulted in internal conflicts, as well. When, in the 1870s, early pastor Thorlaksson wanted to affiliate with the Norwegian Synod, lay leaders of the congregations refused, fearing that the synod "would be in complete control, and we would have no say." The immigrant colony in New Iceland held a two-day community meeting in which religious issues and organization were vigorously (and at times, heatedly) debated. Historian Valdimir Eylands commented, "People who hardly had shelter over their heads and in many cases didn't know where their next meal was coming from, spent two whole days to hear debates on . . . scholarly (religious) themes."

The tendencies toward strong and independent thought within the Icelandic community also led some members of the community toward free and radical thinking, challenging Christian orthodoxy within the congregations. In the 1880s one such Icelander, Björn Pétursson, adopted liberal, Unitarian views, and became the first Unitarian "missionary" to North America, gathering a small following of scattered groups in the upper Midwest. In 1891 Icelandic Synod pastor, Magnús Skaptason, preached a series of sermons calling into question various parts of traditional Christian theology; he was expelled from the synod, and several of his congregations followed him. These elements formed the Icelandic Conference of Unitarian Churches in North America in 1891. Another pastor in the synod, Frederik Bergmann, came under the influence of the new liberal theology during ministerial study in Norway during the 1880s. He soon came into theological conflict with Bjarnason, and in 1909 Bergmann and six congregations left the synod. Eylands commented, "The ardor of the battle led both of these eminent leaders to extreme positions which they no doubt regretted in later life."

Magnús Skaptason

Besides the establishment of congregations, the legacy of the Icelandic Synod is a distinctive form of Lutheranism in North America, where lay people took theological issues seriously and debated them passionately. Although conflict like this can at times be debilitating, it can also be a sign of religious vitality, where ordinary Christian take ownership of the faith once given to them.

MARK GRANQUIST

Colleges and Controversy: Augsburg and St. Olaf

There are two things (among others) that Lutherans seem to enjoy: They are very loyal to their church colleges, and they do relish a good controversy. About 120 years ago, Norwegian Lutherans in the Midwest had the chance to enjoy a great controversy between the supporters of Augsburg College and St. Olaf College. It was such a controversy that it ended up giving birth to an entirely new Lutheran denomination and the division of their relative supporters into two different denominations. First a bit of background about Lutheran colleges, and then to the squabble between the supporters of Augsburg and St. Olaf.

The nineteenth century saw the birth of literally thousands of small, church-related schools, some of which survive to this day as small, liberal arts colleges. Many of these schools originally began as academies, which were really private high schools (as much of public education ended at eighth grade). A few of these academies still exist in their original form, such as Oak Grove Lutheran School in Fargo, North Dakota, and Minnehaha Academy in Minneapolis, Minnesota. As public education expanded in the twentieth century, some of these academies grew into undergraduate colleges while others eventually closed their doors for good. Lutherans founded dozens of such schools in the Midwest, and most of the Lutheran colleges that we have today grew out of such roots. It was a point of pride for Lutheran denominations that they had "their school," and Lutherans supported them with great enthusiasm—which leads to our controversy.

In the late nineteenth century, there were numbers of distinct Norwegian Lutheran denominations in the United States, as many as five different ones at one time. As the century rolled to an end, great efforts were made to merge these ethnic denominations together, a difficult task made more difficult by thirty years of theological dispute and also by the issue of schools. In the late 1880s several denominations of Norwegian-American Lutherans were engaged in a merger process that eventually led to the formation of the United Norwegian Lutheran Church (1890-1917). Mergers are difficult things to arrange, and this one was complicated by the question of schools, in this case, Augsburg and St. Olaf. The new denomination had to decide the school issue, especially because it was felt that they could only support one such institution.

On the face of it, the problem seemed manageable. Augsburg was primarily an institution for training Lutheran pastors, while St. Olaf was a liberal arts academy and college which trained students for a wide variety of careers. Simple, it would seem: St. Olaf would be the school of the new denomination, while Augsburg would be its seminary. But things are never as simple as they seem, and deeply felt opinions about the nature of church-related education soon came to the fore, erupting into fierce controversy.

Augsburg College was founded first, in 1869, as an institution for training Lutheran pastors for Norwegian congregations in America. Powered by the educational vision of its two primary leaders, Georg Sverdrup and Sven Oftedal, Augsburg grew into a coordinated, nine-year course of education for young men—academy to college to seminary. St Olaf was founded in 1874 by B. J. Muus and others, first as an academy, then as a college, which was co-educational from the beginning and which sought to prepare young Norwegian-Americans for a variety of positions in the world (including the ministry).

Sven Oftedal

Georg Sverdrup

Bernt Julius Muus

When the United Church was founded in 1890, many saw the academy and college portions of Augsburg as being superfluous, and long-term support for them was ambiguous, at best. Supporters of Augsburg saw church support for St. Olaf as a threat to their vision of a coordinated theological education, and the battle began. In good Lutheran fashion it involved spirited letters and articles in the press, fights in church conventions, secret meetings, and even disputes in the Minnesota legislature and the state courts. As Richard Solberg summarized the debate, "Friends of Augsburg assailed St. Olaf for its humanism and rationalism, its 'luxurious facilities,' its doctors of philosophy, its masters of art, and [its] deficits. St. Olaf supporters branded Augsburg as a 'humbug' institution offering piety as a substitute for intellectual rigor and scholarship" (*Lutheran Higher Education in America*, 232).

St. Olaf's School's first student body, 1875

Augsburg College Old Main

As it turned out, in 1893 the supporters of Augsburg formed a group of supportive congregations, the Friends of Augsburg, which eventually became a separate denomination in 1897—the Lutheran Free Church. As a failed attempt to reconcile the Augsburg supporters, St. Olaf was cut free from the United Church in 1893 and led a precarious life until it was reclaimed by the United Church in 1899. Both colleges survive to this day, and their athletic teams compete in the same conference. How many of their fans realize that the roots of rivalry go back to church controversies of the 1890s!

MARK GRANQUIST

Thea Rønning: One Life Among Many

Thea Rønning

What can one person do or accomplish in the short time that is allotted to humans on earth? Millions of people are born, live, and die; grieved by family and friends, they quickly become only a memory. Thea Rønning was one such person. She lived at the end of the nineteenth century for only thirty-two years, and now, except for the patient research of a historian, would be totally forgotten. But the story of Thea's brief life needs to be remembered, especially as an example of the thousands of other young American Lutherans who heard the call of God.

Thea Rønning was born into a pious farming family in Norway in 1865. She received a limited education and was confirmed in 1880. Greatly influenced by the Pietist revivals of her day, in 1887 Thea discovered that God had work for her, although the exact nature of her call only gradually unfolded. Together with her brother, Nils, and other young Norwegians, Thea immigrated to the United States in 1887, settling in southern Minnesota. The voyage to the new world was rough and exhausting, and the United States was a strange and disconcerting place. But Thea and Nils soon located their older brother, Halvor, and found themselves a home among the Norwegian-American community.

At this time, many Christians in Europe and North America were gripped by the call to take the Christian gospel to the people of Africa and Asia. Thousands of young Christians left everything behind to go to the mission fields, and not a few of them died tragically young in this calling. The call to mission work swept through the congregations, Ladies Aid societies, mission societies, Sunday schools, academies, and colleges of Norwegian America. Young people heard God's call to go to places like Madagascar, South Africa, India, and China. Thea and Halvor discovered their call to China, made possible by the newly formed China Mission Society. In 1891, brother and sister joined a larger group headed to the mission field and, after another arduous journey, arrived in China on December 1, 1891.

Objectively, they had no business going to China. They were poor, they knew no Chinese at all, and it was a very dangerous place, with its rampant disease and starvation, not to mention the political instability and violence. But they had a deep love and confidence in their Savior, a trust in God's providence (in life and in death), and immense concern for the spiritual and physical welfare of the Chinese people.

Thea and Halvor Rønning

Thea and Halvor eventually settled with other missionaries in Fancheng, an inland area of northern China. They learned Chinese and made contact with local people. Women missionaries such as Thea were very important, for the initial approach toward many Chinese families was through the women, to whom only they could gain access. Although Thea was personally used to poverty, the wretched condition of many of the Chinese women appalled her; grinding poverty and disease were combined with brutality, including female infanticide and footbinding. Thea sent letters back to her sponsoring communities. In one from 1895 she described her work:

> I have been stronger this winter than before. It is very difficult to be sick and to study this difficult language. We have forty girls in our girls' school. . . . Now we have started to make house calls and then we really discover need. We talk to the women and children about God. It is so new they cannot fathom it, but God's Spirit has power and can open the heathen heart.[1]

Life on the mission field was not all trial, however, and in some letters she describes her joys and successes, as well as the challenges. She found her own personal joy through her marriage to another missionary, Carl Landahl, in late 1896.

---

1 Gracia Grindahl, *Thea Rønning: Young Woman on a Mission* (Minneapolis: Lutheran University Press, 2012), 146–47.

This missionary work often came at quite a personal sacrifice, and too many of them paid the ultimate cost, dying on the mission field. Thea herself suffered several life-threatening illnesses, and on March 23, 1898, she died at the age of thirty-two.

The church in Taipingdian, China, where Thea Rønning served

Despite wars, upheavals, and persecution, Western Christian missionaries continued their work in China through the first half of the twentieth century, but after the Chinese communists came to power in 1949, they were expelled. For the next forty years very little was known about the fate of Christianity in China and whether it would survive at all. With the opening up of China in the past thirty years, there has been a remarkable resurgence of indigenous Chinese Christianity. Estimates now range between 50 and 150 million Chinese Christians, with a substantial rate of growth. Even with all the trauma, Christianity has taken root and is growing. None of this could have happened without the efforts of Thea and thousands of others who risked all to answer God's call. Thea's was a life well lived.

MARK GRANQUIST

Reindeer and Hunger and Hope: Brevig Mission and Shishmaref Lutheran Churches

There had been years of famine in the land. For the Inupiaq, an indigenous people living north of Nome, Alaska, and south of the Arctic Circle, hunger gripped them in the early 1890s. A government leader and teacher, Sheldon Jackson, suggested that introducing reindeer and reindeer husbandry into these communities might alleviate their suffering. Herds of reindeer were located across the Bering Strait in Siberia. It was also known that Laplanders from the northern regions of Norway had the expertise and the skills needed to make the plan work. A hungry people, a herd of reindeer, a government official, and Laplanders, three continents and a variety of languages and cultures—it's the stuff of legend; it's the stuff of mission and the work of the Holy Spirit. A recipe for a church plant? Not yet! It was the spiritual needs of the Laplanders which sent the call out to seminarians training at Luther Seminary in St. Paul, "We need a pastor!" So across the plains of Montana in a train carrying Pastor T. L. Brevig, his Norwegian bride

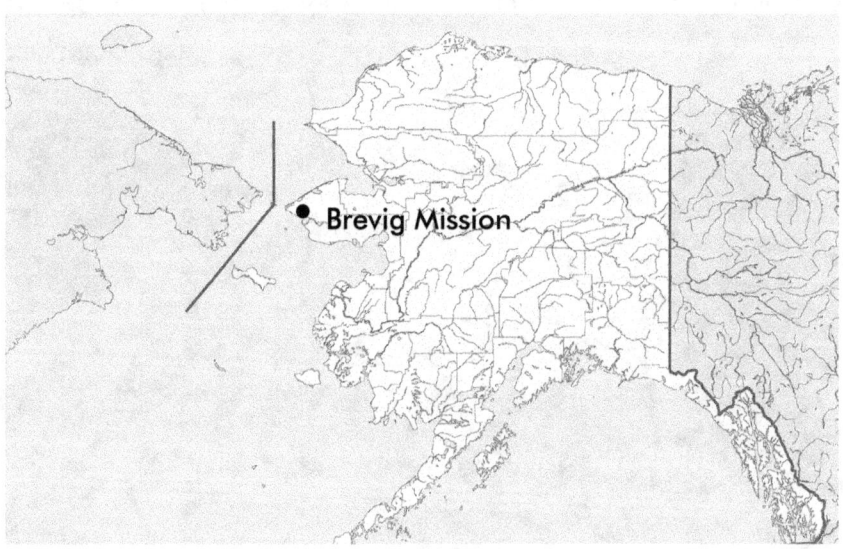

Julia, a group of Lapland reindeer herders, and a Lutheran deaconess left to meet the hunger of a community on the banks of the Tuxuk and the Bering Sea. This place became Brevig Mission, Alaska, where the first (old) American Lutheran Church (ALC) congregation in that state began in 1894.

The T. L. Brevig Family

Almost ninety years later in 1983, a just married, newly ordained clergy couple left to serve among the Inupiaq community birthed from the intersection of reindeer and hunger and the gospel. Elsie Kugzruk, born upriver in an umiak (boat) remembered the missionaries gathering the colorful Lapland reindeer herders into a wall tent singing songs in an unfamiliar language. She told me, one of those newly minted pastors, that story and described the scene in which she was just a child, outside the tent looking in: Strangers had entered into her world, uninvited(?), a vibrant established Inupiaq community, armed with a faith, the gospel and the skills of reindeer husbandry.

A flu epidemic ravaged the villages of the Seward Peninsula in the years between 1914 and 1918. Trained deaconesses, nurses, young women of faith were called to tend to the orphaned children left behind. Sister Anna Huseth, Sister Helen Frost, and many others raised the children, tended to the sick, and cared for the spiritual needs of these young Inupiaq at the orphanage in Brevig Mission.

Helen Frost

Anna Huseth

Long before words like *cross-cultural* and *multicultural* became fields of study and intent, Brevig Mission and Igloo, Alaska, were a study in cross-cultural ministry. Many of the Inupiaq elders in the village shared stories of these women who taught them to sing hymns in their first language, Norwegian, and to knit colorful gloves and mittens in the patterns brought with them from Norway and Denmark.

This context is a snapshot of the development of leadership among women in the immigrant Lutheran churches. It was the cry and vision of Sister Anna Huseth and the missionary zeal of the newly formed Lutheran Daughters of the Reformation (LDR) that planted the church in Shishmaref, Alaska, in the late 1920s and early 1930s. Sister Anna knew that there was an entire village that had not heard the gospel of Jesus Christ. On one of her furloughs, she met with the young women of the church and the church leaders (at that time only men) and told them of the need for a church in Shishmaref. Out of the offerings of the women, funds were secured to build a church and call a pastor.

Now, almost 120 years later, the communities of faith—in Nome and Teller, Brevig Mission and Wales, Shishmaref and Alaska Native in Anchorage—proclaim the gospel in English and Inupiaq and continue to nurture leaders for their villages and towns and cities and state. Polar bears are harder to find, and the warming of the ice cap means the ocean is rising and taking back the once-thriving village of Shishmaref. A forced migration of people is leaving this island for Brevig Mission and Nome and Anchorage. The role of the church has emerged as the primary tool in helping to preserve the Inupiaq language and culture through the translation of hymns and the exploration of new forms of worship which include traditional dance and drumming. Young adults shaped in these communities of faith have taken on the challenge of governing their communities for future generations.

SUSAN TJORNEHOJ

Shishmaref Lutheran Church today

Come to the WELS!
Wisconsin Evangelical Lutheran Synod

The English word "synod" is derived from a Greek word that means "going the same way." In the early church, synod meant a meeting where bishops from a regional area met to discuss theological and organizational issues. In Protestantism, synods were conceived of as a permanent way for pastors and congregations to organize themselves. When Lutherans in America began to form congregations, they  followed this pattern. Though the first two organizations were called by the term "ministerium" (gathering of ministers), the lay leaders of the congregations soon demanded and got representation; thus the gatherings of clergy and congregational representatives were called synods. Individual pastors and congregations voluntarily associated with a given synod, but while belonging to that organization they were bound by its communal decisions. The term "synod" however can take on two different meanings among Lutherans in America: it can mean either a regional or a national body. In the Evangelical Lutheran Church in America synods are regional parts of the whole; there are sixty-five synods in the ELCA. However, the term "synod" can also refer to a national church body, such as the Lutheran Church–Missouri Synod (LCMS) or the Wisconsin Evangelical Lutheran Synod (WELS), which both have congregations in many states across the country.

The Wisconsin Evangelical Lutheran Synod began as a regional synod in Wisconsin, but over its history has grown to include congregations in forty-seven American states and four Canadian provinces, with almost 1,300 congregations and nearly 400,000 members. By means of merger and expansion, it is the third largest Lutheran denomination in North America, although much smaller than either the ELCA or LCMS.

WELS has its roots in the German Evangelical Ministerium of Wisconsin, founded in 1850 by German Lutheran pastors in that state. When it was incorporated in that state in 1864, they added the word "Lutheran" to its title. In German immigrant communities in the United States there was often a mixture of Lutherans and Reformed (Calvinist) Protestants, and often cooperative efforts developed. But the Wisconsin Synod became increasingly conservative and exclusively Lutheran, especially as it came into contact with other American Lutheran groups who were not as strict as it had become. The question that developed between Lutheran groups concerned fellowship or cooperation with other Christian groups, especially the amount of theological agreement that had to be reached before such fellowship could be allowed. The Wisconsin Synod, along with the Missouri Synod, took on a very strict position on fellowship; to them it meant complete agreement on all points of doctrine and practice. These two groups had grave doubts about whether other American Lutheran groups were orthodox enough, and in 1872 Missouri and Wisconsin formed a new cooperative organization along these lines, the Synodical Conference.

In 1892 the Wisconsin Synod affiliated with the Michigan and Minnesota Synods. In 1917 this group, along with the Nebraska Synod, formed the Evangelical Lutheran Joint Synod of Wisconsin and Other States. In 1959 the name was changed to the present Wisconsin Evangelical Lutheran Synod. In the twentieth century, the WELS has grown into a national denomination, though still roughly half of its members and congregations are located in the state of Wisconsin and even more in contiguous states such as Michigan and Minnesota. After World War II, the WELS leadership became increasingly worried about what they saw as "liberal" trends within the Missouri Synod, which created conflict within the Synodical Conference. WELS broke fellowship with Missouri in 1961, and today it is only in fellowship with several other, very small Lutheran groups.

WELS takes the question of fellowship very seriously, wishing to avoid any hint of cooperation with any other religious (or quasi-religious) groups with which they have not negotiated a theological agreement, so they have no interaction with local ecumenical religious groups or even most other Lutherans. They shun fraternal groups, such as the Masons, Elks, Moose, or Odd Fellows, and even discourage their children from joining the Boy Scouts or Girl Scouts because of religious concerns. The WELS has an extensive network of private, parochial schools—334 elementary schools and twenty-three high schools, as well as two colleges and a seminary, with a total of 41,000 students. They see this network as necessary to assure that their children are educated in the orthodox Lutheran faith and to assure that they have church leaders and pastors in the same mold.

Though WELS was traditionally located in the Upper Midwest, it has actively spread into southern and western states, where it has established mission congregations. A number of LCMS members and even some congregations have left Missouri in the 1970s and 1980s to affiliate with WELS. WELS has also been active in mission outreach—in the United States with the Apache Indian Mission in Arizona, and missions in Africa, Asia, and Latin America.

MARK GRANQUIST

Emmy Evald: A Vision for Women's Leadership

"Emmy Evald was a Tartar," Lois Englund told me when I learned that she actually had known this remarkable, best-known Swedish-American woman of her generation. So it is not surprising that one of Emmy's best known lines, certain to provoke the Augustana Lutheran Church women to action, was: "The pastors are against us!" Most of us know that women can get a contrarian reputation just by saying what they think out loud. Emmy Carlsson Evald (1857-1946) was not dismayed by this kind of resistance, however. Instead of submitting, or stifling herself, she spoke right through it so that others could express themselves and experience the power of making things happen. She was one of the most remarkable Lutheran women in American history.

Emmy Evald

Working primarily within the Swedish Lutheran Augustana Synod, Emmy organized a Women's Missionary Society in 1892, creating an active force that extended the sphere women's work at home to faraway places among women and children in India, China, and Africa. With her able leadership, the Augustana Women's Missionary Society continued to grow in strength and leadership clout. Organized in congregational, conference, and synodical levels, it trained women to lead meetings, speak in public, design programs, raise money, recruit members, research and write articles, and promote a cause. The successor organizations for women in the churches are built on Emmy Evald's pioneering leadership.

Emmy Evald first learned at home, where her mother was a vital force and a model for extending the resources of their parsonage home to many needy people in the bustling immigrant neighborhood around Immanuel Lutheran Church, where Emmy's father, Erland Carlsson was the pastor. In 1870, together with her older sister Annie, Emmy left home to get an education in Sweden, where her mother and father had many friends and supporters, and where interesting innovations in women's education were occurring. Annie and Emmy attended Mamsell Cecilia Fryxell's Rostad (a place of rest) School, in Kalmar, Sweden. This school educated girls in a home environment, where their special gifts and capacities were nurtured through Mother Fryxell's attentive and loving guidance. Annie and Emmy's experience at this school was an immersion in the revival, missionary-oriented ethos of the Swedish religious movement that had shaped their father in his early youth and ministry. At Rostad, industry, order, and simplicity were the qualities each young woman was to develop.

In her active adult years Emmy and her family sought to replicate this model of home and education. Her parents created their own Rostad, giving this name to their country home outside Lindsborg, Kansas. In 1892 the women—wives of pastors and lay delegates attending the synod meeting—met separately to organize the women's missionary society for the Augustana Synod. Rostad was a place of inspiration that helped Emmy form a close society of women who were dedicated to advancing the kingdom of Christ in this world.

Augustana's Women's Missionary Society worked together to lift up the concerns of women around the world. In order to meet the increasing needs in the church's broadening mission fields, women heard the call to become teachers, nurses, doctors, and homemakers. American women going out to the mission field needed professional training, and the existing female academies in the United States had to be retooled in order to meet

The Executive Committee of the Augustana Women's Missionary Society, with Evald front and center

these demands. When the Women's Missionary Society was asked to raise the funds for a women's dormitory at Augustana College, where a lack of suitable housing for women on campus discouraged applicants, the women set to work raising significant funds. Their ideal conception of an appropriate home for women students ran into opposition from the male-led college board of directors who locked horns with Emmy and the society. They then responded with a petition drive and writing campaign. Thanks to that media blitz, we know what they were up against. When the women lost their battle and the dormitory was to be constructed near an auto dump, they nevertheless fulfilled their pledge and funded an opulent, grand and spacious building.

Emmy Evald had a vision for women's education that pointed toward service and leadership. In the schools and colleges where young women study today, the model of success is personal and individualistic; students are taught to strive to win in a competitive environment. Elements that inspired Emmy's achievement and that she employed to create a cohesive body of women leaders are more difficult for us to achieve. Competitive models encourage change through provocation and tolerate high levels of conflict and friction. Competition leaves little time for the patient relationship building that fashions sustainable communities. Emmy's model of education would push us to develop ways to identify and nurture personal talent and character and in this way encourage the ideals and dreams of young people.

Emmy Evald

MARIA ERLING

Bold Woman Day

Women of the Evangelical Lutheran Church in America designates an annual Sunday in February to recognize "women who are bold, women who take risks on account of the gospel, women who believe more boldly still in Jesus Christ." Unattached to a dramatic event or historic meeting, not linked to an influential leader or a high-profile project, the day provides an excellent starting place for considering the ministry of thousands of women's organizations in American Lutheran churches. These organizations—including local ladies' aid groups, the Hauge Synod Mission Dove, the Lutheran Free Church Women's Missionary Federation, and the Joint Synod of Ohio Women's Missionary Conference—cultivated and were guided by remarkable women whose leadership multiplied the steady work of a multitude of members.

Lutheran women's organizations founded in the late nineteenth and early twentieth century had much in common with other Protestant women's groups of the time. These Christian women came together regularly for prayer and study, for companionship, and to share in various projects. Sometimes they met in the church, but often they met in one another's homes, admiring and enjoying the hostess' culinary skills. By the turn of the century local groups were federated into national bodies that sponsored missionaries, supported charitable intuitions, and produced educational materials.

Like Methodists and Presbyterians, Lutheran women in Pennsylvania, North Carolina, and Wisconsin, in General Synod, Iowa Synod, and Augustana Synod congregations gathered to support their congregations' ministries and one another. Since the second wave of Lutheran immigration to the United States from Scandinavia and Germany coincided with these developments, some women's groups were founded prior to their congregations. The women's organizations functioned as mothers of the congregations.

Nothing in Luther's Small Catechism exempted women from either receiving God's grace or excused them from the admonitions to love their neighbors; nonetheless most congregations prohibited them

A Ladies Aid at the Lutheran church in Crane Creek, Iowa, 1903

from voting, and no Lutheran church ordained women. Although many of their members might not have recognized it, these groups were part of the woman's rights movement that flourished in the same years. Just as advocates of woman's suffrage insisted that all citizens were entitled to the responsibility of voting, these Lutheran women insisted on being active participants in the church and its work.

Among immigrants of that time, women were central to establishing new churches in an unfamiliar setting. In the state-supported, folk-churches they left behind, membership had been assumed. In the United States things were different. Here church membership was voluntary; there were many sorts of churches to choose from; and all of them needed to be self-supporting. By their volunteer work and their fund raising, women helped forge a more participatory understanding of church membership, more suitable to American conditions.

While the specifics in each group varied, there were general patterns and common activities such as an annual mission festival featuring a visit from a missionary. He would preach and tell about his work in India or China or Madagascar. Women prepared the several hearty congregational meals. They provided the handcrafted items auctioned to raise funds.

Once the clean up was complete, the women continued to support the missionary. Through correspondence and updates in church publications, they stayed in touch with him, with his family, and with their church community. In these ways women fostered an

Lutheran Ladies Aid in Mercer, North Dakota, 1916

expansive, global sense of the church knit together by personal relationships, informed prayer, and financial support. They understood that the church extended beyond their congregation and circled the world.

The church also was closer to home, of course. In those early decades each social ministry or charitable institution managed its own finances, rather than depending upon a unified national church budget. When cash was in short supply, rural pastors received bushels of apples, baskets of eggs, and loaves of bread to supplement their salaries. Similarly women's groups sent gifts in kind to orphanages and homes for seniors, to hospitals and schools operated by Lutherans. The jars of jam and bushels of potatoes, bed linens and curtains bound the women who sent them to the work being done in those places. They were partners in these ministries where faith was active in love.

In their congregations, women's work extended their activities in their homes: feeding and cleaning and teaching. Confirmation records suggest that their basic theological knowledge was comparable to their brothers' in kind and at least as good, if not better, in quality. Women with musical gifts could lead the congregation from the keyboard or by directing a choir. In general, however, their opportunities for formal leadership in the congregation were limited to the women's organization or with children.

Women were able to exercise influence on congregational matters even without having a vote. If the women who had raised the funds judged that an organ or a furnace was more needed than some other item, the organ or the furnace was what would be purchased. This strategy allowed women a voice in the body. It recognized that women played an essential role to the congregation's life and work. However, it also promoted an unhealthy linkage of financial contributions to decision making. Certainly the body of Christ is not intended to do the bidding of those who have money.

Within their own organizations women both offered one another support and cultivated their own leadership. In some instances the pastor attended their monthly meetings to lead the Bible study and offer prayers. Some men thought women incapable of doing these things, while others feared that, once women assumed these responsibilities, they would come to desire others as well. Most often women took the lead themselves. Frequently the pastor's wife was the founder of the local group, and many served as officers in the federated societies. By the mid-twentieth century the national organizations provided instruction that encouraged any woman to prepare Bible study or chair a meeting.

The changes in women's lives beyond the churches were also evident within Lutheran women's organizations. Once there had been a North Aid and a South Aid with membership determined by geography. Later circles might be organized for young mothers or for professional women. Bible studies continued, but new programs also turned members' attention to social conditions that restricted women's lives. Today women have opportunities to take public leadership, both lay and ordained.

Without these women's efforts many Lutheran congregations and social ministries would have done less, and their work would have been less effective. Their lives remind us the central truths about church membership—that is active with responsibilities to worship, to learn, to give support. It is local, but it is also in a church with ministry that includes works of love extending around the world.

L. DEANE LAGERQUIST

Lutherans Go Latin: Hispanic Lutheranism

It all started with a Swedish-American theological student from Rock Island, Illinois, who in 1898 decided that the people of Puerto Rico needed to hear the Lutheran proclamation of the gospel. Never mind that he himself had only been in America for nine years, that he was not ordained, and had no official or financial backing—no, he was going to Puerto Rico. And one other thing—he didn't know a word of Spanish. But Gustav Swensson traveled to Puerto Rico, learned the language quickly, and began to preach in San Juan in 1899, the beginnings of Spanish- and Portuguese-speaking Lutheranism that now counts over one million Lutherans in Latin America, and tens of thousands of Hispanic Lutherans in the United States.

There had been Lutherans in Latin America for centuries—not in Spanish or Portuguese territories, but in the Virgin Islands and Guyana. In the nineteenth century, European Lutherans began to immigrate to South America, especially Brazil, Argentina, and Chile, and founded Lutheran congregations there. But they founded immigrant congregations in their immigrant languages, especially in German. Though they lived in countries that spoke Spanish or Portuguese, they did not initially consider an outreach to their neighbors who used those languages. Mission work, it seems, was proper to Africa and Asia, but not to Latin America.

All this changed in the twentieth century. Swensson's initial efforts in Puerto Rico were taken over by one American Lutheran group, while another started a mission in Argentina in 1908, and a third began in Columbia and Bolivia in the 1930s. In the 1940s and 1950s, American Lutherans began serious efforts to reach out to Latin American populations in over eighteen countries in the region. And the descendants of European Lutherans in Latin America began to make the transition to the use of Spanish or Portuguese within their communities, and to reach out themselves to the local populations. After World War II, there was a serious growth of Lutheranism

Missionaries and Puerto Rican church leaders, c. 1915

and Lutheran churches in Latin America, which soon became autonomous and independent of their mission sponsors.

Spanish-speaking Lutheranism in Mexico and the United States actually began north of the border, then was taken back into Mexico by Hispanic converts and American Lutheran missionaries. As early as 1916, a few pastors from the Texas Synod began work among Mexican-Americans in the Rio Grande Valley, which eventually grew into a full-fledged home mission project. The Texas District of the Lutheran Church–Missouri Synod also began outreach to Mexican-Americans there in 1926, and their official records in 1932 list Spanish (Mexican) mission work in Chicago and Los Angeles as well. Both of these were considered "home" missions (rather than foreign missions), and both included the formation of Spanish-speaking congregations as well as Lutheran periodicals, theological books, and worship materials translated into Spanish. The Missouri Synod even established a Spanish-language edition of its popular radio ministry, the *Lutheran Hour*.

It was from these bases in the southern United States that American Lutherans eventually took Lutheranism south of the border into Mexico. Building on earlier efforts among German immigrants to Mexico, the Missouri Synod began mission work in Mexico in 1940 and eventually formed the Lutheran Synod of Mexico. In 1936 Myrtle Nordin of Lake Lillian, Minnesota, who had studied Spanish as an independent missionary in Columbia, gathered a group to form the Latin American Lutheran Mission (LALM). They began outreach with Spanish-speaking populations in south Texas and northern Mexico, forming congregations in Mexico that would eventually form the Evangelical Lutheran Church of Mexico. Beginning in 1945 the World Mission Prayer League began their own mission work in Mexico, leading to the formation of the Lutheran Apostolic Alliance of Mexico (1977). Finally the American Lutheran Church began work in Mexico in 1947, building off the earlier work in south Texas, which led to the formation of the Mexican Lutheran Church (1957). There are currently about 10,000 Lutherans in Mexico itself.

Although a few Hispanic Lutherans in the United States came by way of immigration (notably Puerto Rican Lutherans to New York), most of the Spanish-speaking Lutherans in America converted to Lutheranism while in this country. Outreach to Hispanic Americans had begun early in the twentieth century in Texas (as we have seen), but this work really took off after 1960 or so, with specific and targeted home missions work. By 2000, the Evangelical Lutheran Church in America listed 180 congregations that used Spanish in worship (including those in Puerto Rico), with a total Hispanic membership of over 39,000 people. The Lutheran Church–Missouri Synod listed 120 Hispanic congregations, with 96 "Hispanic workers" on its rolls. Both denominations have special associations or conferences for Hispanic work. With the Hispanic population in the United States growing rapidly, this portion of the population will continue to be an important sector for Lutherans in America.

MARK GRANQUIST

Richard Reusch: Cossack, Scholar, Missionary, Teacher, Pastor

In a seminar room in the Old Main building of Gustavus Adolphus College, St. Peter, Minnesota, are the portraits of a number of retired faculty members. Most of these pictures are generally the same, with the interesting exception of one. In this picture, a rather fierce looking middle-aged man glares out at the world, cradling a heavy shotgun across his chest. This is a portrait of Gustav Otto Richard Gustavovich Reusch (generally called Richard), whose life seems like something out of a sweeping Russian novel. And if perhaps some of the stories about his life are a bit exaggerated, it is certain that if even half of them are true, he lived a very adventurous life.

Richard Reusch

Reusch was born in 1891 in southern Russia, into a family of German Lutheran settlers and grew up in a time of famine, plagues, and political instability. Some of his family were military officers, while others were pastors and professors, so as a young boy Richard was sent to be educated and trained among the Cossacks in southern Russia, attending a rigorous military academy as a youth and serving with the Cossack regiment on the Persian border. But Reusch eventually decided to take his life in another direction. In 1911 he resigned his commission and headed to the university at Tartu, Estonia. He intended to get a doctorate in history and ancient languages, but was drawn toward preparation for the Lutheran ministry as well. In 1917 anarchy and violence hit Estonia, with German troops battling Communist forces. He was caught up in the chaos and eventually made his way to Germany as a refugee. During this time he developed a deep aversion to the Russian communists, who had killed the emperor to whom he had pledged his loyalty.

From 1919 to 1923 he worked in Germany and Denmark in pastoral roles, but there was nothing permanent for him. He was contacted by the Leipzig Mission Society for missionary work in Tanganyika (Tanzania); this former German colony had been taken over by the British, and German missionaries were not allowed to remain in the country. Seeing that he was a Russian citizen, Reusch would be allowed in the country and could join American missionaries from the Augustana Synod who were trying to maintain the Lutheran mission work. He arrived in East Africa in 1923 and served there as a missionary for the next thirty-one year—four terms through 1954. His early years in Africa were very difficult; the chaos of war had decimated the Lutheran missions, and they were extremely short-handed. By all accounts Reusch did heroic work in the 1920s and 1930s to keep the missions going and growing. The missions were staffed by Swedish and American Lutherans; Germans were later allowed to return, but were driven out again during World War II. The political situation was often very difficult, especially dealing with the British colonial officials.

Reusch's exploits on Africa's highest mountain, Kilimanjaro, became the stuff of legend. He made his first ascent of Kilimanjaro in 1923. During his second ascent in 1926 he found the mummified corpse of a leopard. It was said the photo that he circulated inspired the opening paragraph of Ernest Hemingway's semi-authobiographical work, *The Snows of Kilimanjaro*.

Reusch seemed to thrive on the mission field, and in 1927 he married a nurse missionary from the Augustana Synod, Elveda Bonander, with whom he had several children. While on furlough from their missionary terms in Tanganyika, the Reusch's traveled the United States, speaking at Augustana Lutheran congregations with vivid stories of the mission field, stories that sometimes got more vivid with repeated retellings. Reusch was an avid big game hunter (hence the shotgun), and his story about killing a charging lion with his shotgun never failed to captivate audiences. From his time in the Caucus Mountains, Reusch was also a keen mountaineer, and he climbed Kilimanjaro and other East African peaks many times, helping to survey these mountains. For one ten-month period in 1929 he traveled through the Muslim regions of the Middle East, learning about and reporting on Islam and the peoples of this region. But it was his mission work with the Masai people of East Africa that truly engaged his heart. It is easy to see how these warrior nomads of the African plains would appeal to the former Russian Cossack officer. He spent a great deal of time with them, and continued to raise funds for the Masai mission after he left Africa.

In 1954 the Reusch family left Africa for good. Seeing that he had an advanced degree, he was hired as a professor of religion at Gustavus Adolphus College, where he taught for ten years, until retirement in 1964. Former students have commented on what a remarkable figure he was on campus. After his retirement from teaching, he became the pastor of a small Lutheran congregation in Stacy, Minnesota, where he served until his death in 1975.

Reusch the explorer and mountaineer

To say that Reusch had an adventurous life would be an understatement. But it was his loyal service to God and the Lutheran church that he would probably claim as his chief accomplishment.

MARK GRANQUIST

Lutherans and the Lodge

When most people these days think about the term "lodge," their minds most likely picture some rustic main building at a lakeside resort. So when they hear the American Lutherans have, at times, fought long and hard about the "lodge issue," they are rightly confused. But in this case the term "lodge" has nothing to do with summer camp, but is rather a synonym for social, fraternal organizations such as the Masons and many other similar groups that used to be very popular in America. So why did a large swath of American Lutherans decide that being a lodge member was antithetical to being a good Lutheran Christian?

While groups like the Masons, Rosicrucians, and the Illuminati had a long history, back to the Middle Ages (and were in their origins a religious alternative to Christianity), most of these fraternal organizations—such as the Odd-Fellows, Knights of Pythias, and dozens of others—are of nineteenth century origin. By that time, these groups functioned as fraternal societies for men, providing not only a social outlet but also valuable professional contacts and even financial support. Many of these groups were general in nature, while others targeted specific groups of individuals—early labor brotherhoods and college Greek fraternities for example. They were a widespread part of male life in nineteenth and twentieth century America.

Many of these lodges (sometimes referred to as "secret societies") were highly organized, with very detailed and ornamented rituals, complete with secret ceremonies. Some of the groups were organized on a quasi-religious but non-sectarian basis, complete with chaplains and rituals that paralleled and mimicked traditional religious belief. There were generally no doctrinal requirements for membership, and the "brothers" could be from a variety of religious groups, including many forms of Christianity and Judaism, as well as those who were Deists and other forms of "free-thinkers." American Roman Catholics, generally not accepted at the time as members in some of these groups, formed their own parallel fraternal society, the Knights of Columbus.

The major doctrinal issue that some Lutherans had with these "secret societies" was the question of "unionism," or of being in religious fellowship with others without being in doctrinal agreement with them. Many of these groups did have definite religious elements, even if many lodge members ignored or downplayed them, and their membership was often religiously mixed. As one Lutheran critic of the lodges wrote in 1899, "In most of these societies, members join in stated religious rites and exercises conducted by religious officers, chaplains, priests, etc. according to accepted rituals or books of forms." Further, they did these things in mixed religious company. Whether or not you actually believed these rituals or found them religiously persuasive, you were in essence (these critics suggested) worshiping with them.

There was a second, more practical set of issues. In essence, these fraternal groups were competitors to the Christian churches for the time and affiliation of men. Though many members of these secret societies were also members of local congregations, there was often a rivalry and tension between lodge and church. Church members tended to be a majority of women, and it was often a struggle to get men to commit to being active church members. Sometimes the activities and rituals of the lodge could come into conflict with congregational life, especially funerals. As evidence, the *Lutheran Book of Worship* funeral service includes the following warning: "The ceremonies or tributes of social or fraternal societies have no place within the service of the church."

Since these groups were so popular, Lutherans struggled to determine the best approach to dealing with them. In some Lutheran groups, lodge membership was not a major concern, and laymen and even many pastors were members of them. Other Lutheran denominations believed that a pastoral and persuasive approach to the issue was necessary; they would try to convince their members that lodge membership was not proper for good Lutheran Christians, and try to wean them away from the lodges. Still other Lutherans took a firm approach to the issue, suggesting that lodge membership was never allowable, threatening disciplinary action against lodge members in their congregations. It even became an intra-Lutheran issue, with some Lutherans suggesting that other Lutheran were "soft" on the lodge issue.

In the twenty-first century, this issue has faded in importance, primarily because membership in these secret societies has plummeted. Still, it is a concern for some Lutherans, especially the question of divided loyalties and participation in quasi-religious organizations.

MARK GRANQUIST

Praising God in English: Lutherans and the Language Transition

Upon their arrival in North America, European Lutheran emigrants immediately had to face the reality of the English language, spoken by most of the rest of the citizens of the United States and Canada. Like almost all other immigrants, Lutherans initially sought to establish religious institutions in their native languages, but soon had to face the divisive question of whether these institutions should transition to the use of English, and if so, how? Resistance to this language transition was fierce, and it divided homes, congregations, and denominations. However, the pressure to use English was unstoppable, and eventually all Lutheran groups came to the use of English.

The problem was that Lutherans had no models for how Lutheranism might actually be structured in English, and whether this could actually work. The story is told of the old immigrant who allowed that God might indeed be able to understand English, but, he sniffed, "God doesn't LIKE English." In a more serious vein, immigrant Lutherans had serious concerns that Lutheran theology and traditions might not be able to be translated into English with full expression and richness. Also, they had invested heavily in ethnic-language institutions and materials in North America in order to minister to the older generations and to recent immigrants, and they were worried that these valuable ministries might go by the wayside.

German, Swedish, and Dutch Lutherans came to North America during the colonial period of the seventeenth and eighteenth centuries. Like other ethnic immigrants, they founded congregations and parish schools in their native European languages and developed a rich ethnic culture. But the pressure to use English was inevitable, especially as new Americanized generations of Lutherans came along. Since there was only a small Swedish immigration and since it fell off quickly, the Swedes made the initial transition to English, and since there were no other English-speaking Lutherans around, these colonial Swedish congregations became Episcopalian. The Germans

lasted longer, but by about 1820 the transition to English was well accomplished, though not without many bitter fights.

Beginning around 1840, and lasting until the First World War (1914-18), a second, massive wave of European emigration brought millions of new Lutherans to North America. The colonial Lutheran pattern of ethnic-language congregations and institutions was replicated on a much larger scale this time, and American Lutherans developed a rich culture in their ethnic languages, not just congregations and schools, but also hospitals and social service agencies, publishing houses and periodicals, among many others. As long as new immigrants kept coming (and it was hard to see then that they would not continue to come) the necessity of these ethnically-based ministries seemed irrefutable.

And yet the generational tide, and the need to be conversant in English, soon affected these immigrant groups, as well. New generations of younger Lutherans arose that spoke English primarily and understood the ethnic language only imperfectly. Immigrant parents well understood that the route to success for their children was in English, and in many of the Lutheran schools and colleges the primary language of instruction became English by the late nineteenth century. Yet though the immigrants increasingly accommodated English in many areas of their lives, the ethnic languages were maintained in two bastions—the home and the congregation. The battle over the use of English was ferocious, pitting children against their elders. Many younger Lutherans got very little out of worship services and sermons in the immigrant languages; to the young, they might as well be listening to Latin or Greek.

San Francisco News, June 1953.

CHURCH OF THE WEEK — First United Lutheran Church, Geary-blvd at 30th-av, known as "The Church With the Lighted Cross," celebrated its 67th anniversary last Sunday. The church has been known until recent years as First English Church, the name dating back to its origin in 1886, when it was first Lutheran church on the Pacific Coast to use the English language in all its service. Rev. Kenneth E. Hartzheim is newly appointed pastor of the church, which is affiliated with the United Lutheran Synod.

Up until the First World War (1914), the old immigrant languages reigned supreme, but in the next fifteen years they collapsed almost entirely in favor of English. Why this dramatic decline? Anti-German and anti-foreign sentiment during the war spurred many Lutherans to adopt English as a means of showing patriotism. During and after the war, anti-immigration sentiment ran high, causing Congress to dramatically curtail immigration. And finally, the generational tide came in, with second and third generation, English-speaking Lutherans taking control of Lutheran congregations and institutions. American Lutherans began the task of building a Lutheranism in the English language.

This same dynamic is now playing itself out among the ethnic congregations of Lutherans that have come to North America during the third great wave of immigration that began around 1965. Lutheran emigrants from Latin America, Africa, and Asia have formed ethnic-language congregations in North America, and they exhibit many patterns of language development as did the earlier two waves. They are already beginning to struggle with many similar language and cultural issues. If the patterns of the past hold true, they, too, will make the transition to English, and further enrich the mosaic of English-speaking Lutheranism in North America.

MARK GRANQUIST

Red and Green and Black and Blue: Lutheran Hymnals and their Impact

Isn't it rather strange that we American Lutherans tend to refer to the hymnal/worshipbooks they use by the color of their covers? Just gather with any group of Lutherans, and pretty soon they will start talking about, and critiquing, the hymnals that they have used in their life. "Why, I remember the old _____ (insert your favorite color) hymnal. Now, that was a good one. Much better than this new _____ (insert your least favorite color) hymnal that we have now!" Lutherans can get rather passionate about their hymnals, probably because hymns and singing are such a big part of our worship and devotional lives, and changing these things can really stir up controversy. Just think about the emotions raised when our favorite hymns (the ones we know by heart) are changed or deleted from the newest version of the hymnal.

Hymns and hymnals have always been very important in the Lutheran tradition. Luther wrote or re-wrote quite a number of hymns, and the first Lutheran hymnals appeared already in the first decades of the Reformation. The century after Luther was a golden age of hymnody, when the great Lutheran chorale hymns

"Ein Feste Burg" in a hymnal of Luther's time

were written and later re-set by composers like J. S. Bach. The immigrant Lutherans who came to North America, starting in the eighteenth century, customarily brought with them a Bible, the Small Catechism, and the Psalmbook or hymnal of the region of Europe from which they came. In this new country, with few Lutheran congregations or pastors, the immigrants would gather with their hymnals to worship God and give thanks. They used these European hymnals for many years—a link to the world that they had left behind, and a beloved religious resource.

In the eighteenth and nineteenth centuries, things began to change for American Lutheran hymnody in two important ways. First, there was a dramatic surge of new hymns and types of hymns coming out of the Anglo-American world. Revival hymns, gospel hymns, revivals of ancient and medieval hymns, and many others came to enrich the Protestant hymn traditions. These kinds of hymns, often more subjective and personal, were adopted and copied by Lutheran hymn writers out of the Pietist tradition. The second big development was the translation of the Lutheran hymn tradition into English. The Lutheran immigrants began to worship in English, and this stimulated the production of dozens of new American Lutheran hymnals. Of course this shift brought controversy. Which of the traditional Lutheran hymns should be translated and retained in these new hymnals, and how many of the new Anglo-American hymns should be included? Hymnal controversies are nothing new!

With the multiplication of Lutheran denominations in the nineteenth century came ever more and even more varied American Lutheran hymnals. Each new denomination, it seems, had to have its own hymnal. It was important, it seems, for the group identity and sense of purpose of each of these denominations for them to have their unique hymnal, something in common from which they could worship and sing. The same phenomenon worked in reverse, too. Hymnals became an important means by which American Lutherans came together and merged their denominations. The way toward merger was often preceded by the development of a common hymnal: First, get the congregations of the distinct denominations to worship and sing out of a common hymnal, it was reasoned, and the road to merger would be easier. In the later decades of the nineteenth century, the three divided colonial era Lutheran groups adopted a common

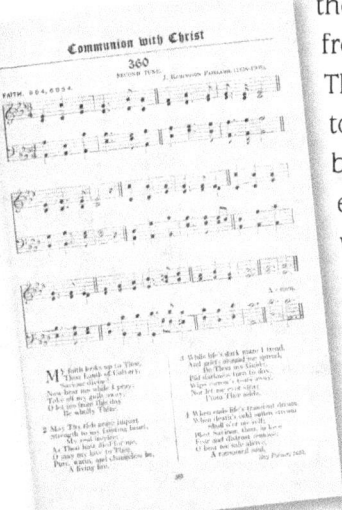

Common Service Book and Hymnal, 1918

Service Book and Hymnal, 1958

hymnal, the *Common Service Book and Hymnal*, which preceded their merger in 1918. Midwestern immigrant German groups came together in 1930, assisted by the American Lutheran hymnal. In the 1950s, eight different American Lutheran groups came together to develop a common hymnal, the red *Service Book and Hymnal*. Although the merger process ended up with two different denominations instead of one (the American Lutheran Church and the Lutheran Church in America), the result was that the majority of American Lutherans were now using a common hymnal. In the 1970s, the development of the green *Lutheran Book of Worship* was envisioned as a common hymnal for all American Lutherans. (This, too, proved too ambitious.)

The late twentieth century saw a further expansion of Lutheran hymnody, with new hymns from Latin America, Africa, and Asia being included in the newest Lutheran hymnals, including the *Evangelical Lutheran Worship* (ELCA), *Lutheran Service Book* (LCMS), and *Christian Worship* (WELS). New hymnals broaden the ways in which Lutherans worship and tie them together with Christians from around the world. Hymnals have had an amazing impact on the culture of American Lutheranism.

Lutheran Book of Worship, 1978

MARK GRANQUIST

Lutherans Learn to Cooperate

By the beginning of the twentieth century, American Lutheranism had grown to be the third largest Protestant family in the United States, after the Baptists and Methodists. Fueled by the arrival of millions of Lutheran immigrants from Europe, there were more than two dozen different Lutheran denominations divided by language and theology. Most wanted to become American and take their rightful place in the American religious scene, but their divisions made them less ineffective on the national level.

During the First World War (1917-18) these Lutherans sought to demonstrate their patriotism and to support the troops, but this required a degree of mutual coordination between the various Lutheran groups that previously had not existed. In 1917 they formed the National Lutheran Commission on Soldiers and Sailors Welfare to raise funds and employ chaplains for the military camps. As that war was winding down in 1918, eight Lutheran denominations formed a more permanent organization, the National Lutheran Council (NLC), to explore more ways in which American Lutheran groups could cooperate and do their work more efficiently. One of the largest Lutheran denominations, the Lutheran Church–Missouri Synod, did not formally join the NLC, but did coordinate some of its efforts with the new group.

There were many things for the NLC to do, things better accomplished in a coordinated fashion rather than separately. Two initial concerns were the support for and reconstruction of war-ravaged Lutheran churches, and support for Lutheran missions in Africa and Asia. It also coordinated many things domestically, including Lutheran efforts in education, social services,

Christmas seals and pins provided not only financial support but also Lutheran identity.

and home mission expansion, as well as services such as planning and publicity. The NLC became a clearinghouse and coordinating center for the great expansion of the work that American Lutherans carried out in the first part of the twentieth century.

During the Second World War (1941-45) the NLC again mobilized American Lutherans for action, to support the troops, coordinate chaplains, provide assistance at home for the workers in the new defense industries, and other similar tasks. During and after this war, it helped sponsor a major fund drive, Lutheran World Action, which raised millions of dollars for war relief. Together with the Lutheran Church–Missouri Synod, the NLC cooperated in a new group, Lutheran World Relief, which shipped over a billion pounds of relief supplies to troubled areas around the world in the twenty years after 1945. The NLC also coordinated the assistance for European Lutheran churches and resettled war refugees in the United States and Canada.

During and after the Second World War, the NLC also broadened its work in North America. Important areas of this service included campus ministry, Lutheran higher education, social welfare services,

Food appeals, this one in Nebraska in 1946, raised funds for fellow Lutherans in Europe, suffering after World War II.

aid to migrants and refugees, and planning and coordination for the massive post-war founding of new Lutheran congregations, especially in the new suburbs and in the growing areas of the south and west. One particular area was the expansion of Lutheran media presence through radio, television, and even movies!

As American Lutherans continued to work together, many thought that this successful cooperation demonstrated the viability of the merger of American Lutheran denominations, and through the 1940s and 1950s merger negotiations gained ground. At this time it proved impossible to get all eight Lutheran groups into a single merged church body, so in 1960 four groups formed the American Lutheran Church (ALC), and in 1962 four others formed the Lutheran Church in America (LCA). These mergers were made possible in part by the relationships and cooperative efforts that had been accomplished by the NLC.

In the early 1960s, the ALC, LCA, and Lutheran Church–Missouri Synod forged even closer working relationships in many of these ministry areas, and by 1966 they had decided to form a new cooperative body, the Lutheran Council in the USA (LCUSA), which took over and expanded many of the functions of the NLC. LCUSA represented an unprecedented level of cooperation between Lutherans in America, representing over ninety-five percent of all American Lutherans. LCUSA also continued and expanded the traditional efforts of the NLC in areas of social service, education and campus ministry, assistance to refugees and immigrants, and many other activities. LCUSA became an important agency for planning and research, for historical and archival preservation, and as the public face of American Lutheranism.

As the ALC and LCA moved toward merger into the Evangelical Lutheran Church in America in 1988, the continuing need for LCUSA was diminished. The new ELCA and the Lutheran Church–Missouri Synod decided that many of LCUSA's functions could now be handled on a bilateral basis between the two denominations or spun off into other groups, so LCUSA came to an end. But these two groups, NLC and LCUSA, played an important role in the larger development of twentieth-century American Lutheranism and its ministries to the nation and the world.

MARK GRANQUIST

Evangelism: Lutherans and "the Boat"

It is fairly common these days to hear American Lutherans lament the numerical stagnation (or decline) in their congregations and denominations. When asked to diagnose the cause of this current malady, it is often suggested that Lutherans are in numerical trouble because they never learned how to do evangelism. When pressed to explain how American Lutheranism got so big in the first place, the response often is, "Lutherans never did evangelism; they simply recruited the immigrants when they got off the boat." This (erroneous) statement is often known as the "myth of the boat." But this myth is wrong. Lutheran immigrants did not automatically flock to Lutheran congregations; they actually were quite resistant. Lutherans had to do quite a bit of hard evangelistic work to draw them in.

The actual numbers of Lutheran immigrants who actually joined Lutheran congregations was rather low. By about 1920, for example, the percentage of Scandinavian-Americans (first and second generation) who were members of Lutheran congregations ranged from about ten percent of the Danes to about thirty percent of the Norwegians. (It is much harder to figure the percentage of Germans, though we can assume it was similar.)

Immigrants entering the U.S. at Ellis Island

Back in the European old-country, the immigrants had no choice but to be Lutheran; here in the United States, they had the freedom to affiliate with any church (or none). The immigrant Lutheran churches were weak, few in number and resources, and chronically short of pastors. Voluntary American religion was also strange to these new immigrants; all this joining and financially supporting a local congregation was quite foreign to them. In retrospect, it is amazing that the American Lutheran congregations grew as much as they did. They grew because American Lutherans actually became pretty good at doing evangelism.

In the colonial period, the initial formation was driven by lay Lutherans who arrived here and founded congregations before there were any Lutheran pastors. Lay Lutherans decided to gather together, recruit their fellow immigrants, establish congregations, and then start searching for a pastor to lead them. As Americans moved west after the Revolutionary War, groups of Lutherans would gather together and form congregations on the frontier, served by itinerant or missionary pastors who would travel between congregations or by ministerial candidates who were in the process of becoming ordained. Occasionally Lutheran missionaries from Europe would work among the Lutherans. (America was for many years a missionary field.)

Zion Lutheran Church, Oldwick, New Jersey

When the great nineteenth-century immigration began in the 1840s (it would continue until World War I began in 1914), the crush of millions of new, non-English-speaking immigrants threatened to overwhelm American Lutheranism. But at great cost and great sacrifice, the new immigrants managed to build congregations, schools, colleges, seminaries, hospitals, and social service agencies. Small groups of Lutherans pulled together and established local congregations. Immigrant pastors scoured the countryside to gather in scattered people. Home missionaries canvased the new territories and rapidly growing cities, and they brought in more people. Pastors, already pushed to their limits, traveled great distances to establish satellite congregations. By 1900 Lutherans grew to become the fourth largest religious family in the United States, with about 2.175 million members.

If the "myth of the boat" were actually true, then Lutheran growth should have leveled off or even stopped after World War I, when the United States severely curtailed immigration. Add to the end of mass immigration the Great Depression and World War II, and the prospects for growth would have seemed to be dim. However, this was not the case. By 1935 the number of Lutherans had more than doubled, to 4.6 million; by 1950 to over 6.1 million, and at its peak in the mid-1960s, American Lutherans numbered over 9 million baptized members. So how did they do it?

Evangelism. By the middle of the twentieth century each Lutheran denomination had a formal apparatus for home mission work and evangelism. Systematically they studied where to plant new congregations and then sent out pastors and lay workers to make them a reality. In the heady period from 1945 to 1965, the Lutheran denominations planted hundreds, if not thousands, of new congregations a year. And local congregations continued their work, too, planting new satellite congregations, especially in the growing suburban areas. Denominational and congregational budgets were stretched to do this work, and pastors worked for minimal wages to make this happen. There was a shared sense of purpose: that to grow the church and bring members to Christ was the most important thing the church could do.

So, it is wrong to say that Lutherans cannot do evangelism. Perhaps it could be said that we have forgotten how to do evangelism, but our history shows that once we were very good at it. And maybe we can learn this once again, beginning by looking to our past.

MARK GRANQUIST

American Lutherans Face War and Depression

In the short space of thirty years, from 1915 to 1945, American Lutherans endured two world wars, a social and economic boom, a crushing economic collapse, and a wrenching process of internal change and rearrangement that dramatically altered the face of Lutheranism in America. And in spite of all the challenges and upheavals, the number of Lutherans in America actually grew in this period of time, from 3.7 million baptized members in 1915, to nearly 5.7 million baptized members in 1945, proving that American Lutheranism can grow, even in the midst of challenges.

Prior to the American involvement in World War I in 1917, American Lutherans were a divided and often isolated group. Though a sizeable segment of Lutherans in North America traced their origins to colonial times (mainly in the east and south), the majority of Lutherans were nineteenth-century Midwestern immigrants, divided into separate ethnic denominations. Some felt a loyalty to fellow Lutherans in Germany, but most Lutherans were isolationist, wanting to keep out of foreign wars. When the United States abruptly entered the war in April 1917, American Lutherans were jolted out of their ethnic cocoons. They faced an eruption of popular sentiment not only against anything German, but also against foreign-ness in general. In the heat of war, American Lutherans jumped to prove their patriotism, very actively supporting the war efforts. Cancelling big pan-Lutheran plans to celebrate the 400th anniversary of the Reformation in October 1917, they organized to provide military chaplaincy for the troops. Cooperative groups, like the National Lutheran Council and the Lutheran Brotherhood, trace their birth to this time.

After World War I, American Lutherans faced rapid changes in society, as well as in their congregations and denominations. Many Lutherans still worshiped in a foreign language, but the war accelerated the switch to English, which effectively happened in the decade of the 1920s. The pressure for consolidation led to three major mergers (in 1917, 1918, and 1930), while most American Lutheran groups were pulled into further conversations about unity. The weakness of European Lutheranism led to a crisis in Lutheran missions around the world, and American Lutherans were called in to lead Asian and African missions "orphaned" by the war. The number of Lutheran congregations in North America grew from 15,000 in 1915 to 16,500 in 1930, along with a similar growth in educational and social service institutions.

The Dust Bowl affected the agrarian economy.

Yet through this period after World War 1, there were worrisome developments. The rapid changes within American Lutheranism, and in the wider society, brought conflict and fear. The vote for women, the "red mence," prohibition, and disputes over evolution, meant constant social ferment. The 1920s saw a disastrous economic decline for American farmers (previewing the greater Depression in the 1930s), problematic for the church because most American Lutherans lived in rural areas. Yet American Lutherans began to think more outside of their own boundaries, participating more in national and international efforts for mission and Christian cooperation.

Many churches set up soup kitchens.

Starting in 1929, the Great Depression of the 1930s was a wrenching challenge to American Lutheranism. The economic crisis of this time meant that the American form of voluntary religion suffered deeply; Lutheran congregations saw a dramatic drop in money, and Lutheran pastors often went without pay. Though there were greatly increased needs for religious and social services,

Lutheran denominations and institutions, seeing benevolent giving drop by one-half, had dramatically fewer resources. There was also a "spiritual depression" in the United States, as attendance at worship and participation in religious activities also declined. Some Lutheran educational and social service institutions closed their doors during this time, and the rest struggled to survive.

As the world situation worsened during the 1930s, American Lutherans remained politically isolationist, strongly feeling that America should stay out of European affairs; there even was a small pacifist movement among them. Yet with the Nazi invasions of Denmark and Norway in 1940 and then Pearl Harbor in 1941, American Lutherans once again jumped full throttle into supporting the American war effort. They pulled together pastors and resources to minister to overseas troops and to large new communities of defense workers, while trying to maintain the life of their own congregations. In 1945, by the end of World War II, total North American Lutheranism had grown to over five million members. Because of their efforts in evangelism and mission, and in spite of the challenges of the past thirty years, they had emerged as a much stronger religious force in their North American communities.

MARK GRANQUIST

The Last Voyage of the Zam Zam

It has never been easy to be a missionary—to move from one's home and go into a new (and often very different) culture, to have to learn new languages and eat new foods. Many missionaries have struggled with their health in regions with unfamiliar diseases, uncertain sanitation, and limited medical facilities. Especially in the nineteenth century, more than a few missionaries to Africa and Asia (and members of their families) died while on the mission fields. To these regular risks were added further dangers from war, insurrections, political instability, and other societal ills. However, few stories are as dramatic as the story of a group of missionaries (including some American Lutherans) who survived the sinking of the ship *Zam Zam* in the south Atlantic during World War II, on April 17, 1941.

The events of the two world wars brought havoc to Christian missions in Africa and Asia. Since many of the countries in these two continents were under European colonial rule, the conflicts between the European countries rippled out in waves. Caught up in the war, missionaries from one side were interned by the colonial powers of the other side, while missionaries from neutral countries were cut off from the support of their homelands. The missionary efforts of all suffered, and in some places churches, schools, and hospitals run by the missionaries had to be abandoned. Christians in America often had to step in and support these so-called "orphaned missions," since America was less often directly affected by the events in Europe.

When World War II broke out in 1939, there were 172 German Lutheran missionaries in the British colony of Tanganyika (now Tanzania) who were interned in camps, and their institutions were abandoned. The Swedish-American Augustana Synod, who already had a few missionaries in the country, stepped forward to provide missionary personnel for these orphaned missions. After a mad scramble to recruit new missionaries, the Augustana Synod's Board of Foreign Missions faced a difficult issue: How, in the midst of a world war, could they transport eight adults and nineteen children to Africa? A neutral ship, the *Zam Zam* of Egyptian registry, left America in March 1941 with 144 American missionaries on board, including those from the Augustana Synod. The ship's route took it down past Brazil and around the southern tip of Africa, although it never made it that far. Mistaking it for a British troopship, the German raider *Atlantis* intercepted the *Zam Zam* in the South Atlantic on April 21, 1941, and sank the ship. By some miracle none of the passengers or crew of the *Zam Zam* were killed, though several were badly injured. The survivors were taken aboard another German vessel, the *Dresden*.

Conditions aboard the prison ship were very bad: The ship was severely overcrowded, the men were separated from their families, and there was very little food. The Germans were not sure what to do with all these prisoners, and the ship wandered around the Atlantic Ocean for a month. Finally the German captain took a bold move; he risked the British blockade and landed safely in occupied France on May 19, 1941. Ironically, that same day the (erroneous) news was broadcast that the *Zam Zam* had been sunk, and all passengers were assumed to be lost. It was not until the next day that the survival of the passengers and crew was confirmed.

The *Zam Zam* just before its final voyage. American missionaries from the Augustana Synod were on board.

The *Zam Zam* ten minutes after being shelled by a Nazi raider ship, the *Atlantis*. Passengers are fleeing the sinking ship on life boats.

The ordeal was not over for the passengers of the *Zam Zam*. Since the United States was still at this point neutral, the American citizens were eventually transported through Spain to Portugal, and from there to the United States. There were also a significant number of Canadian citizens on board, and as enemy non-combatants they were interned in Germany until the end of the war, often in very difficult conditions. After the Americans returned home, some of the survivors volunteered to try to reach Africa again, and they did in 1942. Other American Lutheran missionaries also later made it to Africa unharmed, even though wartime conditions remained very dangerous. The Lutheran efforts in Tanganyika were continued, and on this base the autonomous Lutheran church in independent post-war Tanzania was born, which now numbers over 5.3 million members.

Survivors from the *Zam Zam* were taken aboard the rescue ship, the *Dresden*. They were finally delivered to a French port after a month aboard the ship.

Though the voyage of the *Zam Zam* was a dramatic moment in the history of American Lutheran mission work, it was only one example of the dangers that missionaries faced. Many others faced similar dangers during World War II, including American Lutherans who were interned in terrible conditions by the Japanese forces in Asia. But they faced these traumas with a steadfast faith that the God who had called them to service would keep them safe. They risked all to share the good news of Jesus Christ to others around the world.

MARK GRANQUIST

American Lutheran Aid to Refugees

Though World War II in Europe ended in the spring of 1945, the people of that continent were living in perilous conditions. The war had been one the first modern examples of "total" warfare, which brought the destruction of combat to all sectors of society, not just the battlefield. The lives and homes of many Europeans had been seriously disrupted; millions were without employment, housing, and food; and untold numbers of people had been displaced. Many Germans had abandoned cities destroyed by bombing and fighting, while countless Europeans (mostly from the east) had fled the advance of Russian troops and the Soviet takeover of the Baltic countries and Eastern Europe.

The Frauenkirke in Dresden was largely destroyed by Allied bombing during World War II.

The only major industrial power left, which had not been directly subject to the destruction of war, was the United States, but it was unclear how this country would act. Directly after World War I, the American people and their leaders had largely retreated from the world into a blanket of isolationism. But after World War II, Americans came to realize that if they wanted a peaceful world, they would have to assist the rebuilding of war-torn countries in Europe and Asia; and so they did.

During the war itself, many groups in the United States had already begun to plan for post-war relief and reconstruction. Ready to take their place in this task were American Lutherans, especially in aid to their fellow Lutherans in Europe, as well as others. As early as 1940, American Lutheran groups began major annual fund drives to collect resources for these tasks, and in the decades to come they would raise almost $250 million dollars.

Almost as soon as the fighting ended in Europe, American Lutheran leaders headed there to assess the situation and to begin funneling aid to the people of that continent. Organizationally, the National Lutheran Council (and in cooperation, the Lutheran Church–Missouri Synod) began to work with European Lutheran leaders, eventually constituting the Lutheran World Federation (LWF) in 1947. One of this group's first tasks was refugee assistance and resettlement (Service to Refugees). The situation among the European Lutherans, especially in Germany, was grave, as the war had destroyed churches and other institutions, scattered pastors and church leaders, while the horrors of Nazism and total warfare had scarred the people. Lutherans from the east had fled the expansion of Soviet communism, and were refugees in Western Europe.

Children in a Displaced Persons camp after the war are fed through the services of Lutheran World Relief.

After first meeting the basic needs of people, American Lutheran relief personnel began to work with the Allied Military Government in Germany to plan for the rebuilding of the German Lutheran churches, and to assist in building churches-in-exile for Eastern European Lutherans. Individual Lutheran pastors and others began to work in camps directly with refugees (Displaced Persons, or DPs), and to begin to help them rebuild their spiritual lives and communities. By the late 1940s there was a major Lutheran organization in Europe to coordinate this work, with an equally large organization in the

United States to support and to fund it. In 1948, the United States government passed legislation to allow for up to 200,000 of these displaced persons to enter the United States, a figure that would later be expanded. This was the beginning of a refugee resettlement program, mainly to North America, that required both funding and organization to make it work.

In 1954 American Lutherans founded the Lutheran Refugee Service (now Lutheran Immigration and Refugee Services—LIRS) to coordinate this work. Lutheran congregations throughout the United States were called upon to help resettle the DPs in their communities, and to support them in building new lives in North America. Many congregations responded generously and opened their arms to the refugees. By the 1960s it was estimated that American Lutherans had helped resettle 70,000 refugees in the United States, as well as 22,000 in Canada and 20,000 in Australia.

As this task of resettling DPs from Europe wound down, it became clear that this service to refugees (and immigrants) would be a long-standing and permanent need. Wars and conflicts around the world continued to produce refugees; in the 1960s and 1970s, LIRS worked to resettle refugees from Asia, especially Southeast Asia, and more recently they have worked with refugees and immigrants from Africa. American Lutherans took their place, in many instances took the lead in this work, and continue to support the work of assistance through LIRS, ministering to the continuing needs of a conflicted world and those people affected by it.

MARK GRANQUIST

Courageous Journeys: Lutheran Immigration and Refugee Service

Courage defines the migrants and refugees Lutheran Immigration and Refugee Service (LIRS) is privileged to walk alongside. And defining the moment over seventy-five years ago that inspired LIRS's ministry of mercy and justice was courage as much as faithfulness. U.S. Lutherans concerned about displaced Lutherans in Europe could not sit by idly as conflict leading to World War II swept the European continent. Ralph Long, president of the National Lutheran Council, declared in his 1938 annual report that the displacement of Lutherans in Europe was "a tragic thing to which we dare not close our eyes or remain indifferent." The concern of U.S. Lutherans, said Long, "must be translated into constructive and cooperative assistance."

And so, in the spirit of cooperative and constructive assistance, efforts to resettle displaced Lutherans began as the National Lutheran Council launched Lutheran Resettlement Service in 1939. Who better, after all, to accompany newcomers setting down roots than members of a church made up mainly of immigrants? In the agency's first year of operation, 522 people were resettled by Lutheran congregations and volunteers.

Cordelia Cox served as resettlement director and Clarence E. Krumbholz as executive secretary of Lutheran Resettlement Service.

Refugees arriving in New York by ship were greeted with enthusiastic welcome and details about next steps in their journey. The volunteers also brought sandwiches for the journey, a small but touching detail recounted fondly by former refugees. New arrivals then headed by bus for Pennsylvania or Minnesota or other states where Lutheran congregations were waiting to help them rebuild their lives.

By the late 1950s, the displaced persons and refugees from WWII were mostly settled. Lutheran Refugee Service could have said a prayer of thanks and closed its doors. But in this world fraught with persecution and strife, wars and rumors of wars, sadly there were more tragic things to which Lutherans dared not close their eyes. And after twenty years of serving courageous newcomers, the agency had developed expertise that could help other refugee populations. Networks of ministries to care for people had been created, and strong partnership was forged with the federal government, which provided major financial support.

What began as help for the Lutheran family in a time of crisis actually equipped the young ministry for a much broader mission of mercy and justice for sojourners in peril. In 1960 Lutheran Refugee Service officially began resettling refugees of all nationalities. For at least the last half-century, it also has been helping uprooted people who come to the U.S. directly for protection. Experiencing similar circumstances as refugees, they apply for protection through other immigration statuses like asylum or special visas such as those for victims of trafficking. And so "Immigration" was added to the agency's name, becoming Lutheran Immigration and Refugee Service (LIRS). LIRS in the mid-1970s began working with migrant children who were separated from family by placing them in specialized foster care. Less than ten years later, LIRS observed children seeking safety from conflict in Central America, and it developed efforts to care for them. Also during the 1980s, LIRS became increasingly concerned about torture survivors and other vulnerable people in immigration detention.

Today, LIRS also has a strong network of legal service partners and visitation ministry volunteers working with persons who are in immigration detention for documentation and protection issues, and it advocates boldly for alternatives to detention.

Central to all the care provided by LIRS and its partners is the core belief that migrants and refugees are courageous change agents in their own lives. LIRS walks alongside with practical support when the journey is rough. It encourages and equips people to become not only self-sufficient but also connected and contributing members of their adopted communities. Strangers welcomed in Christ's name become neighbors, friends, and leaders helping communities prosper.

Also integral to LIRS's approach is the spirit of collaboration. It takes a range of connections to walk alongside migrants and refugees. The partnership of Lutheran church bodies has remained steadfast. These church bodies collaborate on vital projects that extend  mercy and speak out for justice. Leaders and lay persons from all three churches volunteer in ways that faithfully show God's love for their new neighbors—through policy advocacy, mentoring, visiting immigrants in detention, becoming foster parents for migrant and refugee children, and financial support.

Collaboration with the federal government is a critical part of LIRS's mission. The U.S. president determines how many refugees will be admitted each year. The administration plus Congress are responsible for funding and for laws governing immigration as a form of humanitarian relief. LIRS implements several State Department-funded programs that protect and integrate vulnerable newcomers.

LIRS celebrated seventy-five years of service in 2014—not simply the anniversary of an institution but rather a commemoration of faithful work by the wider Lutheran community to care for the uprooted in Christ's name. In those years, the LIRS network of social ministries, congregations, families, and countless individuals helped more than 500,000 vulnerable sojourners rebuild their lives in freedom, safety, and dignity.

TARA MULDER

Lutherans from the Baltic

The Baltic countries of Estonia, Latvia, and Lithuania have a history of Lutheranism going back to the Protestant Reformation of the sixteenth century. This region was the last area of Europe to be christianized, which occurred in areas as late as the fourteenth century, often by means of crusading warrior monks known as the Teutonic knights. The German influence in this region meant that Lutheranism began to infiltrate the region as early as the 1520s, especially in the cities. Lutheranism took root in the region during the sixteenth century, especially in the two northern countries, Estonia and Latvia, and among German settlers in Lithuania. Though the Roman Catholic counter-Reformation challenged the Lutheran movement, the Swedish occupation of Estonia and Latvia in the seventeenth century meant that Lutheranism in those countries was officially established by the state; Lutheranism in Lithuania remained a minority group within a decidedly Roman Catholic country. Starting in the eighteenth century, Russia came to control all the countries of this region; the Lutherans were generally allowed to maintain their own congregations and church structures, but sometimes only with difficulty.

Immigrants to North America from the Baltic region began to come rather late in the nineteenth century, settling in the East and

The Baltic States

Midwest, especially in industrial and mining areas where there were jobs. Baltic Lutherans tended to be scattered around the country and had few, if any, pastors to lead them. Established American Lutheran denominations began to reach out to these scattered Baltic Lutherans in the 1890s, but were limited by language barriers. In 1896 the Missouri Synod ordained a Latvian pastor, Hans Rebane, who began to minister to widely scattered populations of Latvians and Estonians, from Boston to South Dakota and up into Canada. Augmented by a newly-arrived Latvian ministerial colleague, they formed Lutheran congregations within the Missouri Synod as a "foreign-language" mission of that church. The Lutheran Ministerium of Pennsylvania also sponsored outreach to Latvians in New York, Philadelphia, and Boston through the efforts of two immigrant pastors, Peter and John Steik. Eastern districts of the Missouri Synod sponsored Lithuanian Lutheran pastors and congregations, also on the East coast, beginning in 1907. A few scattered Estonian, Latvian, and Lithuanian Lutheran congregations were formed in North America, but there were not enough of them to form their own distinct Lutheran denominations, and these congregations continued to be supported by and attached to existing Lutheran groups.

Hans Rebane

With the dissolution of the Russian Empire in 1917, Estonia, Latvia, and Lithuania became independent countries in their own rights, and, although the Russian communists attempted to force them into the Soviet Union, they resisted this pressure. Freed from Russian control, the Baltic Lutheran churches gained strength and moved toward a new national identity. This window of independence was short-lived, however, and in 1940 the Russian army invaded the Baltic countries and made them a part of the Soviet Union. The German invasion of Russia in 1941 brought the region temporarily under German occupation, but the Russians regained control in 1944. Significant numbers of Estonian, Latvians, and Lithuanians fled their countries in advance of the Russian troops and became refugees in Germany and Sweden, where they formed ethnic Lutheran communities in exile. Displaced Baltic Lutheran pastors served their populations in the refugee camps in Germany, and, when these refugees began to be resettled outside of Germany, the pastors followed, and formed ethnic congregations. Many Baltic refugees settled in the United States and Canada after World War II, and new ethnic congregations—Estonian, Latvian, and Lithuanian—were formed in North America. To serve the scattered congregations in North America, South America, Australia, and Europe, they formed ethnic Lutheran churches "in exile," which became part of the Lutheran World Federation. Currently, the Estonian Evangelical Lutheran Church Abroad, headquartered in Sweden, has about 9,000 members in congregations in North America; the Latvian Evangelical Lutheran Church Abroad has about 12,000 members in North America; and the Lithuanian Lutheran Church in the Diaspora has about 5,000 members in North America.

These ethnic Baltic Lutheran congregations in North America served as both an ethnic haven for the refugees, and a way to transition to their new countries. Although many refugees had hopes of returning to their home countries someday, the Russian occupation made this impossible. When the Baltic countries declared their independence again after the fall of the Soviet Union in 1991, relations were re-established between the churches abroad and their Lutheran counterparts in the Baltic, which had suffered greatly under communist rule. These diaspora Baltic Lutherans have attempted to help restore Lutheranism in the Baltic countries, but there have also been tensions between these groups—in Latvia, for example, over the question of the ordination of women. Baltic Lutherans in North America are yet another part of the Lutheran mosaic on this continent.

MARK GRANQUIST

"The Church May Not Just Doze:" Confessing in Indonesia

A dozen Indonesian churches belong to the Lutheran World Federation (LWF). These Lutherans are a minority within a minority. Protestant Christians are the second largest of the five religions recognized by the government of Indonesia; nonetheless, together with Roman Catholics they constitute only about ten percent of the population. Hindus and Buddhists number less than five percent. The vast majority of Indonesians are Muslims.

In this context the Lutheran impulse toward confession generated a new statement, rather than merely affirming sixteenth-century documents. Introducing its Confession of Faith (1951), the Huria Kristen Batak Protestant (HKBP) church asserted: "Therefore the church may not just doze, content with former confessions, but rather in every age must renew and reform them." Citing examples from the early church, the Reformation, and the Barmen Declaration (1934), its authors set out to establish their faith, oppose heresy, and provide a basis for cooperation with other Christians.

As elsewhere in Asia, Christianity was carried to Indonesian first by traders, likely from Persia and India. They were motivated by desire for commercial exchange more than evangelistic zeal. The same overlapping, and yet sometimes conflicting, interests characterized the Portuguese Catholics who arrived in 1511 and the Dutch Protestants who replaced them later in the century. During the 200 years the Dutch East Indian Company controlled trade, it excluded Catholics and restricted Protestant missions.

When the trading company went bankrupt, just as the nineteenth century was turning, the Dutch government assumed responsibility. Both Catholics and Protestant were alert to new opportunities for evangelism opened by the government's policy of religious freedom. Dutch, British, American, and German missionaries were sent to work at various locations on the several islands.

The German Rhenish Mission (RMG) sent Ludwig Nommensen to the Toba Batak people in North Sumatra. He arrived in 1862 and labored there until his death in 1918. During those decades, he saw much fruit from his collaboration with German pastor, Peter Heinrich Johannsen, and Raja Pontas Lumbantobing, an early Batak convert.

Ludwig Nommensen

A recent history of Christianity in Indonesia observed that they suggested that "[n]ew life in Christ could penetrate and renew, rather than annihilate and destroy, the traditional world of the Batak" (page 542). Nommensen's interaction with Batak people involved serious dialogue more than polemical assertions.

Early opposition to Christianity prompted establishment of a Christian village, *Huta Dame* (Village of Peace). Soon, however, the number of Christians increased enough that they could remain in their homes. From the outset schools were an important element of the mission. Self-reliant congregations were the goal.

Nommensen's linguistic facility and his astute negotiation of the interaction between Christianity and Batak customs, or *adat*, contributed to his leadership. Generally he accommodated previous practices, though he opposed ancestor worship. The church order he devised provided a liturgy, governance, and guidance for behavior.

Among his linguistic accomplishments was translating the New Testament and Luther's Small Catechism into Batak, both accomplished in 1874. These choices may have reflected Nommensen's largely Lutheran training.

The RMG's confessional position encompassed the evangelical Lutheran as well as the Calvinist Reformed streams of the sixteenth-century Reformation. Both contributed to the development of independent Batak churches and are evident in the HKBP's confession.

By the early twentieth century, Batak Christians were moving toward independence. During World War I, when German missionaries were interned by the Dutch, the Batak assumed greater leadership. In 1930 the HKBP was organized as autonomous body, nearly two decades before Indonesian won political independence. Since then the HKBP has been active in global and regional ecumenism and several other churches have been formed.

In the 1950s Ephorus (presiding bishop) Justinus Sihombing guided the HKBP into the LWF. Unlike other LWF members the HKBP did not subscribe explicitly to the Augsburg Confession. Instead, emulating the reformers, it wrote its own confession. In it the church demonstrated its affirmation of Lutheran teaching and addressed the context of twentieth century Indonesia.

Like the Augsburg Confession, the HKBP Confession makes positive statements of faith and rejects false teaching. Positive statements highlight what is shared among Christians, providing the basis of cooperation. In agreement with the Augsburg Confession, article eight identifies the gospel and sacraments as marks of the church. The addition of church discipline shows the influence of the Reformed tradition.

The Confession also distinguishes the HKBP from other Christians—such as Adventists, Pentecostals, and Catholics—and from Animists, Muslims, and various secular ideologies. For example, it rejects traditional Batak beliefs regarding ancestors and opposes the view that poverty is the cause of sin.

Affirming the ultimate authority of Scripture, the HKBP declares that its confession is subject to examination. In doing so its members commits themselves to stay awake: to engage with the customs and culture of their time and place, and to ongoing Reformation for the sake of the gospel.

L. DEANE LAGERQUIST

The Story of Two Lutheran Mergers

Without a doubt, the twentieth century for American Lutherans was a century of merger. From over a dozen different major Lutheran denominations (not counting many smaller ones) in 1900 to two major denominations at the close of the century, Lutherans spent the twentieth century merging. Fifty years ago, Lutherans were celebrating the completion of two major mergers bringing together eight different Lutheran denominations—the American Lutheran Church (ALC, 1960-1988) and the Lutheran Church in America (LCA, 1962-1988). But the road to these unions was neither quick nor smooth.

These two mergers were preceded by three mergers in the early part of the century. Eastern Lutherans (from the colonial "Muhlenberg" tradition) had reunited in 1918 to form the United Lutheran Church in America (ULCA, 1918-1962). The majority of Norwegian-American Lutherans overcame their differences to merge together in 1917, forming the Evangelical Lutheran Church (ELC, 1917-1960).

Procession at the Norwegian American Lutheran Church (NLCA) Constituting Convention, 1917. In 1946 the NLCA changed its name to the Evangelical Lutheran Church.

And four Midwestern German denominations, the Ohio, Iowa, Buffalo, and Texas Synods, worked out a merger in 1930, forming the American Lutheran Church (ALC, 1930-1960). These three denominations—along with the Augustana Synod (Swedish), United Evangelical Luther-

A detail from the ULCA Constituting Convention, 1918

an Church (Danish), American Evangelical Lutheran Church (Danish), Suomi Synod (Finnish), and the Lutheran Free Church (Norwegian)—cooperated in an association called the National Lutheran Council (NLC).

Even before these mergers were completed, American Lutherans began to explore the possibilities of further unification. By the 1920s, the immigrant Lutherans were quickly making the transition to English, greatly lessening the need for separate linguistic denominations. This was the age of consolidation in many areas of American life, including the great American corporations and large Protestant mergers. Many Lutherans hoped that a united Lutheran denomination would strengthen their outreach to the world, and show the power of their influence. (Lutherans had become the fourth-largest Protestant family in the United States.) But how was such a further merger to be accomplished, and who would be invited to the table?

Though merger discussions began in the 1920s, they languished through the Great Depression and World War II. After the war the pace of discussions quickened, though huge obstacles remained, especially around the degree of theological unanimity required to achieve merger. The eastern Lutheran ULCA held to unity in essentials only, while the Missouri Synod insisted on complete doctrinal agreement before fellowship or merger. These two large Lutheran groups defined the borders of merger negotiation, while the seven other, smaller groups positioned themselves in between. Which direction should these seven Lutheran groups go? If the ULCA was included in negotiations, Missouri likely would not participate. If Missouri was included, it would only work if the ULCA was excluded. Through the late 1940s and the early 1950s, the Lutheran merger dance was a complicated balancing act of competing positions and ideas.

Finally in 1952, the whole process collapsed. The Augustana Synod (Swedes), historically close to some of the eastern Lutheran groups, decided to walk out of merger negotiations that had excluded the ULCA, leaving behind the ELC (Norwegians), the Midwest Germans (ALC), and others. From here there were two different merger negotiations:

1. ULCA, Augustana, Suomi (Finns), and the AELC (Danes)
2. ELC and Lutheran Free (Norwegian), UELC (Danes), and ALC (Germans)

Missouri declined to participate in either merger process.

Once these merger processes got rolling, they moved to form two large Lutheran denominations, each in excess of two million members. The first, in 1960, was the American Lutheran Church (1960-1988), which consisted of the ELC, the "old" ALC (Germans), and the UELC. The Norwegian Lutheran Free Church eventually came into the merger in 1963, after a bruising round of congregational voting. The Lutheran Church in America was formed in 1962, consisting of the ULCA, Augustana, Suomi, and the AELC.

At the 1960 Constituting Convention of the American Lutheran Church, the assembly marched from the Convention Center, where they were meeting, to Central Lutheran Church for worship.

The outcome of this process was deeply problematic to many people. On the surface of things, it was hard for many to see why there should be two mergers and not one, while others were upset that Missouri did not participate in either process. But others were heartened that the number of Lutheran denominations was now at least reduced to three—the LCA, the ALC, and the Missouri Synod. Optimism ran high in some quarters that this was just another step toward the formation of a single Lutheran denomination in the United States.

Yet it never happened. And the great expectations of the benefits of merger never materialized, either. American Lutherans in 1962 numbered around eight million members. In 2012 these numbers have declined to around 7.4 million members, even while the population of the United States has doubled. Merger has not brought either the growth or the influence for which its proponents had hoped, even with the formation of the ELCA in 1988, bringing together the LCA and ALC, along with a portion of congregations that had left Missouri.

MARK GRANQUIST

Polity and Piety: The Association of Free Lutheran Congregations 1962-2012

Thief River Falls may seem like an unlikely location for a national church convention, but it was there that the Association of Free Lutheran Congregations (AFLC) was organized over fifty years ago. The approximately 300 people who gathered there in October 1962 were almost all members of Lutheran Free Church (LFC) congregations, a church fellowship that finally approved (after three church-wide referendums) a merger with the American Lutheran Church, initially organized in 1960. The LFC decision in February 1963 had been approved by more than a two-thirds majority, in an unusual system that gave congregations 1-10 votes according to membership. Yet almost forty percent of the congregations had voted against the merger, and a concerned minority was committed to continuing the free Lutheran movement.

The Lutheran Free Church, a Norwegian-American church body, was organized in 1897 during a decade of revolt and revival. Centered at Augsburg Seminary in Minneapolis and led by Professors Georg Sverdrup and Sven Oftedal, the revolt sought to maintain a distinctive system of pastoral training and to resist a new synodical structure that was perceived as authoritarian. In the midst of the painful and divisive conflict, many of the congregations were stirred during a powerful season of spiritual awakening, reminiscent of the Haugen movement in Norway.

Originally more of a movement than a structured denomination, the LFC operated for over sixty years under the *Guiding Principles and Rules for Work*, the first of which stated: "According to the Word of God, the congregation is the right form of the Kingdom of God on earth." This form of polity was strictly congregational, not synodical, and was seen as unique among American Lutherans. A delegate system for the annual conferences was not adopted until 1959-60! Yet the founders also spoke of *free and living* congregations, emphasizing that polity was not an end in itself, but rather a means (the best means, they believed) to the upbuilding of spiritual life.

"Despite its disavowal of the synodical type of polity, the LFC more and more functioned like other Lutheran church bodies," wrote Eugene Fevold in his authorized history. A new generation emerged that saw the LFC simply as one of several smaller Lutheran denominations, whose destiny could best be fulfilled in a union with other Lutherans. But those who organized as the AFLC in 1962 wished to continue the distinctive *polity* and *piety* of the LFC. They feared the loss of congregational freedom in the new church body and seemed to discern a growing "high-church" spirit. Some expressed the concern that LFC congregations, primarily less formal in worship style, might be pressured toward uniformity in liturgical practice. Some resisted a requirement in the new church for district presidents to sign pastoral letters of call.

Piety, the second area of concern, may be broadly defined as an emphasis on personal spiritual life. A post-Reformation movement in Lutheran Germany known as Pietism spread to the Scandinavian countries and, with the immigrants, to America, promoting a "living" Christianity with a rich devotional life, a personal witness of faith with a stress on evangelism that would give birth to Lutheran world missions, a strong social concern, and a consecrated Christian walk. The founders of the AFLC believed that there was a growing toleration of "worldliness" within American Lutheranism, and that there was a place for a "wholesome" pietism to be emphasized.

Another aspect of the concern for piety was theological. Opponents of the merger were alarmed that the ALC was a member of the World Council of Churches, which represented a liberal ecumenism to them. There was also a growing awareness that a newer approach to Holy Scripture, called "neo-Lutheranism" by historian E. Clifford Nelson, was gaining a foothold in the Lutheran colleges and seminaries, challenging the "old Lutheran" confidence in the Bible as the infallible and inerrant Word of God.

The AFLC has grown from the original forty to fifty congregations to a worldwide fellowship of 280 congregations in the U.S. and Canada, with mission partnerships in Mexico, Brazil, India, Ecuador, and Uganda, plus missionaries on loan to other organizations. A theological seminary and a Bible institute share a spacious campus in suburban Plymouth with the national headquarters, where the various AFLC ministries maintain offices. The Parish Education department publishes a complete Sunday school curriculum and Bible study materials, and a monthly magazine, *The Lutheran Ambassador*, is an important link between the congregations.

One of our LFC forefathers described his church as "a venture of faith . . . an attempt to build an effective and orderly Christian fellowship with a minimum of human organization . . . an experiment in extreme ecclesiastical democracy." The AFLC continues to be committed to this vision, convinced that there is still a place within twenty-first century Lutheranism for an emphasis on free and living congregations.

ROBERT L. LEE

Franklin Clark Fry: "Mr. Protestant"

Very rarely, if ever, has an American Lutheran graced the cover of an American news magazine. If they have, it was not because they were Lutherans, but because of something else. Famous Lutherans, like Justice William Rehnquist or Senator Paul Simon, might be recognized, but that they were Lutherans was purely incidental. But on April 7, 1958, readers of *Time* magazine were greeted by a cover and feature story focused on Dr. Franklin Clark Fry, the president of the United Lutheran Church in America. The title of the cover and accompanying article designated Fry as "Mr. Protestant." National recognition for a Lutheran leader—quite the surprise! But then, Fry was quite a remarkable man.

Franklin Clark Fry was born August 30, 1900, in Bethlehem, Pennsylvania. Both his father and grandfather were prominent Lutheran pastors, so it was not surprising that Franklin would follow in their footsteps. After graduating from the Lutheran seminary in Philadelphia in 1925, he was ordained as a pastor in the United Lutheran Church in America (ULCA), one of the largest Lutheran denominations in America at the time. While serving for fifteen years (1929-44) as a pastor of a prominent Lutheran congregation in Akron, Ohio, Fry became very active in the ULCA, serving on various church boards and commissions, including its Executive Board from 1942 to 1944.

Franklin Clark Fry

Already a rising star in the ULCA, Fry was elected president of that denomination in 1944. At age forty-four he was very young to be the leader of a major Protestant denomination, but his leadership skills and acumen were readily apparent, and he was would serve as an important Lutheran leader for the next twenty-four years, until his death in 1968. Fry was renowned for his administrative and diplomatic skills: He was very adept in ordering and growing institutions as well as running church meetings and conventions; he was especially a master of parliamentary procedure. In the now-outdated parlance of the times, Fry was a superb "churchman," that is, someone who was devoted to empowering the work of the church by building up and organizing church institutions—boards, committees, ministries, and outreaches. Fry knew how to get people to work together to expand the effectiveness of the Lutheran churches in America and around the world. This was a period in American history where "bigger" was better—bigger businesses, bigger government, bigger institutions—and religious denominations were growing right alongside them. Bigger and more unified meant more effective—a more effective means by which to spread the Christian message.

Fry (left) in the Oval Office with President Kennedy at bill signing

As the leader of the ULCA, Fry was automatically a prominent figure in American and world Lutheranism. He was an important leader in the American Lutheran efforts to rebuild the shattered European Lutheran churches after 1945, and in 1947 he was elected president of Lutheran World Relief, which sought to provide humanitarian assistance around the world. Fry was also instrumental in helping to organize the Lutheran World Federation in 1947 and later served as that organization's president (1957-63). He was also a major leader in the post-war effort to bring about organic Lutheran union in North America. In the 1950s Lutherans were still divided into at least a dozen different denominations; negotiations for Lutheran mergers and unity were complicated, at best. Fry's zeal to bring this about was perhaps an issue; he could be aggressive on this subject, and other Lutheran leaders sometimes did not trust Fry or the ULCA. The merger processes splintered; instead of a single American Lutheran church, by the early 1960s the process yielded two—the American Lutheran Church (ALC) and the Lutheran Church in America (LCA), while the Lutheran Church–Missouri Synod (LCMS) did not join either of them. Fry's denomination merged into the LCA, and Fry served as that group's president from 1962 until his death in 1968. In the 1960s he did manage to get all three major Lutheran denominations to cooperate together in the new Lutheran Council in the USA (1967).

Fry while president of the Lutheran Church in America (center) with Frederick Schiotz, president of the American Lutheran Church (left) and Oliver Harms, president of the Lutheran Church–Missouri Synod (right) at the World's Fair in 1964

Of course, all these intra-Lutheran activities, as impressive as they are, would not have gotten Fry on the cover of *Time* magazine in 1958. But though he was passionately committed to Lutheranism, he was not constrained by its borders. Fry was an instrumental force behind the founding of the National Council of Churches of Christ in the USA in 1950; he encouraged a number of Lutheran denominations to join the new organization and personally served it in a number of different capacities. Similarly, he was influential in forming the World Council of Churches in 1948 and served as chair of its central and executive committees from 1954 to 1968. He was a leading Christian ecumenical leader in the 1950s and 1960s, with a worldwide influence and reputation. Pretty good for a Lutheran pastor from Pennsylvania and truly deserving of a *Time* magazine cover!

MARK GRANQUIST

"Out of Necessity:"
The Church of the Lutheran Confession

If mapped out on paper, the history of the Lutheran church in America resembles a tree with myriad branches. Some branches bend toward each other for a time, and then head a separate way. Sometimes twigs split off forming new branches. The Church of the Lutheran Confession (CLC), a Lutheran body with about eighty congregations or teaching points throughout the United States, celebrated its fiftieth anniversary in 2010. But it traces its history back to the origins of the Lutheran movement. The CLC became its own branch "out of necessity."

In 1872 American Lutheran church bodies often had geographic or ethnic identities; some were allied with a "home" state church, others were opposed. In that year, the Evangelical Lutheran Synodical Conference of North America, or popularly the Synodical Conference, was organized by the Wisconsin Evangelical Lutheran Church (WELS), the Lutheran Church–Missouri Synod (LCMS), the Ohio Synod, and the Norwegian Synod. This new body was to be an expression of the unity of these four church groups. The Slovak Synod joined the Synodical Conference in 1908, and the Evangelical Lutheran Synod joined in 1917. These groups were in full communion, shared educational facilities, did joint mission and benevolence work, and had open pulpit fellowship.

Early on, the Synodical Conference, which held a high regard for fellowship and accountability, struggled with internal disagreements over the doctrine of predestination. But it was in the 1950s that some congregations were challenged to confront what members took as an affront to biblical commitment.In the 1950s concerns arose among several of the synodical partners about stances taken by LCMS, particularly in terms of biblical interpretation. Some saw indications that LCMS was no longer committed to *sola scriptura*, scripture alone. The concerns were so deep, a call for disassociation from the Synodical Conference began to be heard from some pastors and church leaders, especially within WELS.

As David Lau, archivist for the CLC, explained in his recently published history of the CLC, *Out of Necessity: A History of the Church of the Lutheran Confession*:

> In 1955 one of the other synods of the Synodical Conference, the Wisconsin Synod, passed a resolution declaring that the Missouri Synod was causing "divisions and offenses" [from Romans 16:17] contrary to the Word of God. One of their committees said that, because of this, it was necessary to avoid the Missouri Synod because of its toleration of false teaching. In fact, the committee said that if they postponed the decision to avoid the Missouri Synod in 1955, they would be violating the Word of God. But when the matter came to a vote, the Wisconsin Synod voted not to break fellowship with the Missouri Synod.

Over the next few years, a debate arose within WELS concerning the appropriate time and method for ending fellowship with the Missouri Synod. In each instance, action was postponed. Eventually, some then-WELS leaders felt compelled to withdraw participation from a group they saw as in error. Pastor Maynard Witt of Spokane, Washington, first took a stand, saying in 1957, "Out of love to the Wisconsin Synod and out of love and fear of the Word of God, I am compelled to announce my severance of fellowship from the official Wisconsin Synod." Later that year, another WELS leader, seminary professor Edmund Reim, concurred: "I hope and pray that the Synod may yet return to its former ways and to full obedience to the Word of God. I trust that you will realize that I take this step, not in anger, but in deepest sorrow, and because I am constrained by the Word of God."

These statements set in motion developments that led to the forming of a college and seminary in 1959 (Immanuel Lutheran College and Seminary), and a convention to establish a new Lutheran church body in 1960. In August 1960, about seventy-five delegates (forty-two pastors included) met in Watertown, South Dakota, to function as an Interim Conference to determine if there was sufficient common belief to form a joint body. For several years committees had been drawing up documents to approve in order to move forward in common mission. These documents were now put forward for adoption. David Lau states:

Immanuel Lutheran High School, College, and Seminary, Eau Claire, Wisconsin

For a while it looked as though we would not be able to adopt a confession on church fellowship at this convention. There were even charges of false teaching directed towards some of the participants in these debates. But, after more discussion it was realized that the problems was based on misunderstanding.

The confession "Concerning Church Fellowship" was approved unanimously. When voting on the name of the fellowship, Immanuel Lutheran Conference won the first ballot, matching the name of the already existing college. But on the third ballot, Church of the Lutheran Confession received 39 votes to 29 for Immanuel.

BOB HULTEEN

Warren A. Quanbeck: Lutheran Ambassador-At-Large

How did an expert in the New Testament and Luther become a Lutheran ecumenical leader? For at least two reasons. After World War II, U.S. Lutherans played a major role in diaconal, missionary, and refugee work; now they were ready to become involved in wider leadership in the Lutheran world. Around 1960 a new generation of theological leaders was about to step onto the stage. Warren Quanbeck was one of this new generation, but ten years ahead, prepared to take part in this developing American Lutheran role. That was not without its problems. He liked to point out that because he had been cleared of "liberalism" by the Evangelical Lutheran Church's council of district presidents, he was one of the few who could state for sure that he was not a heretic.

Warren Quanbeck

From 1958-1970 he was a member of the LWF Commission on Theology. As such he was directly involved at the LWF Assembly in Helsinki (1963) in the famous or "infamous" statement on justification, which was much maligned by press reports claiming that Lutherans had been unable to agree on their key doctrine of justification. But Quanbeck noted that the Helsinki Assembly actually succeeded in its purpose, which was to place justification in its contemporary theological and cultural context. He was on the Board of Trustees of the LWF Foundation for Interconfessional Research, Strasbourg (1959-1971). At the LWF Assembly in Evian (1970) he was chairman of Section Two, Ecumenical Affairs. From 1971 to 1972 he was the LWF Lutheran Lecturer at Mansfield College, Oxford.

Vatican II

Quanbeck was a LWF delegate observer at the last three of the four sessions of Vatican Council II (1961-1965), in his own words "the single most important theological occurrence of the twentieth century." The observers met weekly for two to three hours with Roman Catholic bishops and staff of the Secretariat for Christian Unity, and they had a definite influence not only on the decree on ecumenism but also on the constitution on the nature of the church. When, immediately after Vatican II, the U.S. Lutheran/Roman Catholic Dialogue began, he was an obvious member. The Catholics challenged us by "running in their first team," he stated, and, because over half of the members had learned to trust each other through contact at Vatican II, the usual maneuvering and hesitation at the start of a dialogue process could be bypassed.

He was a member of the WCC Faith and Order Conferences at Oberlin (1957) and Montreal (1963). From 1958 to 1959 he was tutor at the WCC Ecumenical Institute, Celigny, Switzerland. He was a delegate to the WCC Assembly at Nairobi (1975) and elected there to the Central Committee of the WCC.

This listing, this "ecumenical bibliography," is in no sense complete. Quanbeck was also, for example, a member of the U.S. Lutheran/Presbyterian Dialogue from 1962 to 1966. But what this listing does begin to show is how he became a Lutheran ambassador-at-large. Not only was he directly involved with Lutherans at the world level; he was also involved with Roman Catholics, Anglicans, the Reformed, and, through the WCC, with the Orthodox at the world level. Today, when it is frequently feared that ecumenism is "in a deep freeze" and its future is difficult to discern, it is important to look back two generations to a leader like Quanbeck who, to be sure, was standing on the shoulders of the giants before him, yet who also used his diplomatic skills to build bridges and forge deep personal bonds with other Christian leaders. Then, too, the battles were fierce. Could we trust the Roman Catholics? Would the Orthodox find their way into the ecumenical movement? Where were the Reformed going, anyway? What about apartheid and racism?

At the first official Lutheran World Federation–Roman Catholic consultation, Quanbeck represented the LWF. Here he is pictured with Andre Appel, French Protestant Federation head who would become the LWF general secretary, and William Baum, executive director of the U.S. Bishop's Commission for Ecumenical Affairs

What was needed was trust. What Warren Quanbeck was able to develop, as a kind of Lutheran ambassador-at-large, was the confidence of those he spoke for, the Lutheran leaders who had come to know his work. At the same time he was able to gain the trust of ecumenical partners. It was not simply a matter of endless travel, endless meetings, more debate, and more written statements of agreement. It was most of all a kind of ecumenical perception and integrity, learned and communicated. He wove a net of ecumenical alliances, bridges for wider Lutheran ecumenism.

But he was also a baseball fan, a skilled pianist, a frustrated architect, a social activist, a ready wit. And, not to be forgotten, he was an inspiring teacher (professor of Systematic Theology, Luther Seminary, St. Paul, 1958-1979).

MEG MADSON

A Mining Town Turns Lutheran

On April 1, 1960, Wes Prieb, a student at Seattle's Lutheran Bible Institute, wrote a letter to Howe Sound Company, which owned a mining village in the Cascade Mountains above Lake Chelan, Washington; it was his third inquiry. His letter said: "[Holden's] property might be a desirable place for the use of the church or Lutheran Bible Institute as a summer camp . . . for young people. Information [about asking price] will be deeply appreciated." Howe Sound had replied to Prieb's two earlier inquiries, saying the village was "for sale at $100,000." The company hoped to sell it as a mountain resort, but no buyer had appeared.

The 1960 response was different: Howe Sound would give the property to Lutheran Bible Institute (LBI), asking only that LBI "send a statement saying it had received a gift in the amount of $100,000." When first hearing of this offer, some thought it was

Miners working the mine that became Holden Village

an April Fool's joke. It sounded "phony and a bit ridiculous," said LBI President E. V. Stime. But a couple months later a team, including Prieb and Stime, visited the property; they were impressed by its possibilities and recommended that LBI receive the gift. By December 1960 negotiations with Howe Sound for legal receipt of the gift were finished. Because the town sits on Forest Service land, that federal agency needed to okay its operation as a church facility—and it did.

Youth departments of national Lutheran bodies were then drawn into planning. LBI and youth leaders jointly crafted a purpose statement, saying Holden would be a "center where youth and adults interested in youth may find spiritual, intellectual, and physical renewal for Kingdom service." A permanent Holden board was created, with representatives from LBI and national youth offices; it first met in May 1961. And because LBI declined any permanent responsibility, a separate Holden corporation was created.

An early concern was what to name the enterprise. The mining town had been known simply as "Holden," for the prospector who had discovered ore there in 1896. The new board named it Holden Village: A Place Apart, but to most it was simply Holden Village. It was envisioned initially as a program center for youth and young adults, and the younger generation did provide vital volunteer service during initial restoration work as well as a half-century of service since. But from the beginning Holden has welcomed families and offered program for all generations.

From its start Holden's leadership has been bi-national (Canada and U.S.) and inter-Lutheran. Two of Holden's early on-site leaders came from Lutheran youth leadership, from Minneapolis. Wilton Bergstrand, youth director of the Augustana Lutheran Church, in the summer of 1961 directed nearly fifty work-campers who prepared the village for receiving guests. The next summer he and his wife Dolores gave program leadership for the first guests. Holden's initial executive director was Carroll Hinderlie, a youth director for the Evangelical Lutheran Church. From 1963 to 1977 Carroll and his wife Mary shaped Holden into a center for "hospitality and hilarity inspired by the gospel." Carroll enjoyed noting that a divine challenge

Holden Village

came when "God gave a gift like this to God's least imaginative people—the Lutherans."

And the young man whose letters led to Lutheran inheritance of Holden? When asked what he had hoped his inquiries might accomplish, Wes Prieb would say he never expected Howe Sound to "give the property away, but I hoped they would reduce the price, or some miracle might happen." Wes spent much of his later life there, serving as Holden's PHD (pool hall director) for thirty-two consecutive summers, from 1968 to 1999. He died in early 2000.

Though operated by Lutherans, Holden is known as an ecumenical center for renewal, with a priority focus on faith/society concerns. It is known also as a place of "holy hilarity." Elmer Witt, Missouri Synod pastor who was village director in the 1980s, noted that "Holden is one of very few church-related organizations with the word 'humor' in its incorporation articles."

Through its Lutheran existence, Holden has been acutely aware of living with mine remains. Drainage from inside the mine cavity and ore tailings outside have contaminated the environment. The federal government decades ago declared it a disaster area needing cleanup. Rio Tinto, a large mining corporation, has accepted responsibility for massive mine remediation, which was recently concluded.

Holden during mine remediation

During remediation seasons (May through November) Holden housed workers and volunteers doing village renewal, leaving no room for guests. In 2013 it revised its summer program by including "Holden on the Road" at locales across the continent. Recently Holden launched its "Refresh, Renew, Rejoice" capital campaign seeking $4.8 million. Those gifts will restore Holden's seventy-five-year-old buildings and infrastructure. Fifty-some years after Wes Prieb's April 1 letter, Holden Village continues, a gift serving both church and world. Always, it serves with fun—and that's no joke!

CHARLES P. LUTZ

67

Lutherans Going Public: Should the Church Do Politics?

For much of their history, Lutherans in America have resisted the idea that the church should engage in political action. Individual church members as citizens—Yes! The church collectively—No!

Lutherans overwhelmingly opposed or ignored the "social gospel" movement of the early twentieth century, which sought to "build the kingdom of God on earth" by applying Christian ethics to the social order. But on direct involvement in pursuing social change, Lutheran behavior has since changed dramatically, starting about sixty years ago, when Lutheran bodies began openly supporting the Civil Rights movement. Lutheran statements officially called for segregation's end and federal action pursuing racial justice.

At about the same time, Lutherans also launched formal communication to the U.S. government. The National Lutheran Council opened a Washington public relations office in 1948. Eleven years later, 1959, the NLC issued its first government action proposals, "Toward a Statement of National Policy." The American Lutheran Church (formed in 1960) had a unit for developing social policy positions. The Lutheran Church in America (formed in 1962) did such work through its Social Ministry Board. At its 1971 convention the Lutheran Church–Missouri Synod said that the church is called "to influence . . . institutions such as government, business, and labor, to sensitize them to the task of improving the quality of [human existence]." In 1969 the Missouri Synod issued the very first statement on hunger and public policy among major Lutheran bodies.

All three major Lutheran bodies in 1967 joined as members of a new cooperative vehicle, Lutheran Council in the USA, with an Office of Government Affairs (OGA) in Washington. While LCMS left it in the early 1980s, OGA continued as a public voice for ALC and LCA until the formation of the Evangelical Lutheran Church in America in 1988. The ELCA since then has had offices both in Washington and at the United Nations in New York.

During the period from 1960 to 1990, the three large Lutheran denominations all spoke on public issues consistently: civil rights, world hunger, military draft and Vietnam War, arms race and world peace, South Africa's apartheid system, rural economic crisis, and human sexuality. Some of this was addressed to corporations, and their activities in apartheid South Africa became a determiner for whether church investing would continue in them. Not all Lutheran members were happy about denominational entry into civil life. It

The Civil Rights Movement moved many church members to political action. Here posters are made for the march on Washington, 1963.

struck quite a few as "too political" and unwise "mixing of church and state." The ALC's "Manifesto for Our Nation's Third Century," adopted by its 1976 general convention, responded: "We welcome the continued separation of church and state but deny the separation of religious faith from public life."

Lutheran bodies also sought to distinguish between lobbying and advocacy. The LCA said, in "Advocacy—a Ministry of the Church" (1986): "Both advocates and lobbyists seek to influence public policy and civil legislation. However, advocates exercise moral authority for the sake of others, while lobbyists engage in political and economic pressure for the sake of themselves. Advocates [are] non-partisan champions of justice and the common good."

In the latter half of the 1980s, a most unusual church/state engagement included some Lutherans. It was discovered that government undercover agents were entering congregational gatherings in Arizona to seek information on congregational work with undocumented persons from Central America, leading to possible prosecution of church leaders for federal law violation. The agents presented themselves as supporters of church ministries with undocumented immigrants. In 1986 the ALC, its Alzona parish in Phoenix, plus the Presbyterian Church (USA) and three Presbyterian congregations, filed suit in federal court, claiming that secretive behavior of agents spying on religious gatherings violates the First Amendment prohibition against government interference in the free exercise of religion. With appeals, the judicial process lasted five years. The churches gained a modest victory when the final judgment said:

The government is constitutionally precluded from unbridled and inappropriate covert activity which has as its purpose or objective the abridgment of First Amendment freedoms of those involved. Additionally, the participants involved must adhere scrupulously to the scope and extent of the invitation to participate [in religious gatherings] offered to them.

U.S. Lutherans in the 1980s began public advocacy also with state governments. These offices were launched jointly by ALC and LCA in areas having significant numbers of their members. Under ELCA sponsorship they continue in twenty states.

A recent development, announced in 2015, is a Missouri Synod plan to re-create a formal presence in Washington. LCMS had maintained an Office of Government Information from 1987 until 2000, and its 2015 return was intended to be mainly an educational tool "to serve LCMS interests and those of other conservative Lutherans." It prepares briefs on topics of social concern and provides internship opportunities for young people. Its public policy agenda is limited to three concerns: "life, marriage, and especially religious freedom."

CHARLES P. LUTZ

U.S. Lutherans as Selective Pacifists

Pacifists are persons who, in principle and absolutely, oppose war as a way of resolving conflict. In all of American history, few pacifists have been bred within Lutheranism. It's calculated that, among all major Christian traditions in the U.S., Lutherans have produced proportionately the fewest conscientious objectors (COs). During both world wars of the past century, some of the young Lutherans who did achieve legal CO status felt they must leave Lutheranism because of that church's lack of support for, even hostility to, their stance when called to war.

But a watershed regarding military service came for U.S. Lutherans in the 1960s. Vietnam was this nation's first major military enterprise which large numbers of Lutherans questioned. It became the occasion for the faith tradition to rediscover, reassess, and reaffirm its historic ethical position: that "to have a good conscience before God [the faithful should] neither fight nor serve" in war they believe is against God's will (Martin Luther in "Whether Soldiers Too Can Be Saved").

You could call such Lutherans "selective pacifists." In relation to U.S. draft law, this position became known as "selective conscientious objection" (SCO) and was affirmed by most Christian denominations. All three major Lutheran bodies endorsed it, asking that it be made legal so that, if an SCO were called by the draft, he could do non-combatant service in the military or with a civilian agency. The three major Lutheran church bodies made statements about this stance:

> Lutheran Church in America, 1968: "This church approves provisions whereby persons in the military who become conscientious objectors are permitted reclassification and reassignment [and] urges that these provisions also be extended to the conscientious objector to a particular war."

> Lutheran Church–Missouri Synod, 1969: "Resolved, that the Synod petition the government to grant equal status

under the law to the conscientious objector to a specific war as it does to a conscientious objector to all wars."

American Lutheran Church, 1970: "It is time to amend the [draft law] to provide alternate forms of national service to those who object on religious, moral, and philosophical grounds to participation in a specific war."

While these Lutheran bodies took the same position on selective conscientious objection, not all of their members agreed. There was deep division among the Lutheran faithful which lasted until conscription ended and the war was winding down in 1973. In the ALC a 1972 *Lutheran Standard* article titled "Luther Was an SCO" fed the debate.

These three Lutheran church bodies also joined in funding a Lutheran Selective Service Information office (which this writer was called to staff from 1971 to 1973. It was based in New York City at the Lutheran Council in the USA. And in 1971, the Council's executive director testified to the Senate Armed Services Committee on selective objection. Thomas Spitz, a Missouri Synod pastor, told senators:

Thomas Spitz

> The ethical person is by definition "selective," and is morally answerable for what he chooses. The Lutheran tradition counsels both *selective* participation in and *selective* objection to military service, depending on the circumstances. The criteria for judging flow from the theory of "just war," which has been inherited through Luther from the medieval church and, originally, St. Augustine. Lutheran ethics . . . asserts that moral choices cannot be made cleanly by appeal to some absolute but always are made ambiguously within the vortex of competing claims of such realities as justice and love, liberty and order.

The Senate later voted on writing SCO into the draft law, but only twelve senators favored it.

So, during the entire Vietnam era, young Lutherans who were draft eligible and selective objectors could live in a church that, for the most part, accepted them and tried to minister to them. Those services, almost all conducted ecumenically, included:

- support of draft counseling, much of it through college campus ministries
- visiting draft refusers in federal prisons
- aiding Canadian churches in their ministry to draft exiles
- consulting with military chaplains on ministry to in-service objectors

Lutheran work was not limited to those who said no to military service. It was clear that those who said yes to service in Vietnam and safely returned home were also victims. In April 1973, a Conference on Emotional Needs of Vietnam Veterans was held at the LCMS's Concordia Seminary in St. Louis. Along with veterans, it was attended by health professionals from Veterans Administration and church social service agencies.

Lastly, as the Vietnam chapter was closing, Lutheran churches joined the public campaign seeking amnesty for draft offenders. That federal policy was enacted during the Carter administration in the late 1970s.

The U.S. has had no military conscription for forty years. But our national experience continues calling for "war/conscience" ministry—with those considering military service, those who enter it, and those who survive it. As Pastor Spitz told senators in 1971, the choices Lutherans make about war participation are both "selective" and "ambiguous"—an ideal context for ministry that's "faithful and reforming"!

CHARLES R. LUTZ

Lutherans Seeking Social Change in Racist Alabama Half a Century Ago

It was a Sunday morning in Birmingham, Alabama, fifty years ago. Sunday school at 16th Street Baptist Church had begun. That September 15 morning in 1963 a box of dynamite, planted earlier with a time delay set to detonate after Sunday school opened, exploded under steps near the church basement. Of the twenty-six children in the basement, four were killed.

One of the four black girls who died was Denise McNair, age eleven. Denise was the daughter of a Lutheran lay leader in Birmingham. Chris McNair was Sunday school superintendent and a past president of St. Paul Luther-

The four girls killed in the Birmingham church bombing: Addie Mae Collins, Carole Robertson, Carol Denise McNair, and Cynthia Wesley

an, a Lutheran Church–Missouri Synod congregation. On that fatal morning, Denise was attending the Baptist church with her mother, a member there.

Pastor Joseph Ellwanger of St. Paul Church, who was white, visited the families of all four bombing victims. He expressed amazement "at the ability of the Negro community to continue to love people of the white race."

Planters of the bomb were identified as four members of a Ku Klux Klan group. Three of them were eventually sent to prison—in 1977, 2001, and 2002.

Fifty years ago, Alabama was known as the land of supreme segregation. It had also emerged as the grassroots feeder of a movement, led by church folk, seeking to end segregation. Birmingham, often renamed "Bombingham," was at the heart of that movement.

It's where Martin Luther King Jr., in the spring of 1963, had been jailed after leading nonviolent anti-segregation demonstrations. He then wrote, to white churchmen opposing racial change, his "Letter from a Birmingham Jail."

Seven years earlier, in Alabama's capital, the Baptist preacher with a Lutheran-looking name was leading the Montgomery bus boycott, seeking to end segregation on public transportation. Only one white clergyperson in Montgomery supported King's initial civil-rights activity. He was Pastor Robert Graetz, who served Trinity Lutheran, an all-black (except for the Graetz family) congregation of the old American Lutheran Church.

Robert Graetz with Martin Luther King Jr.

A graduate of Capital (now Trinity Lutheran) Seminary, Columbus, Ohio, in 1955, Graetz began that June at Trinity in Montgomery. There he succeeded another Capital Seminary grad, Nelson Trout, who in the 1980s would become the Western Hemisphere's first black Lutheran bishop.

Graetz had developed a special relationship with Rosa Parks, the initial bus lawbreaker; they lived in the same neighborhood, and she was part of an NAACP group that met at Trinity. Graetz was regularly identified as the only white face at boycott meetings, other than those of media people.

The boycott ended, successfully, in December 1956 with a U.S. Supreme Court decision outlawing segregation in public transportation.

Leaving Montgomery in 1958, Graetz returned to live there in retirement. His three years in Alabama's capital are powerfully described in his 1992 Fortress Press book, *Montgomery: A White Preacher's Memoir*.

More historic actions in Alabama came in spring 1965 in Selma. Dr. King launched protests for voting rights of African-Americans and invited church leaders from across the country to join the demonstrations. For the second protest, on March 9, a thirty-eight-year-old Unitarian Universalist pastor from Boston responded to King's call. He was Jim Reeb. And joining him were many clergy from Minnesota.

One was a Lutheran pastor from Edina, Griffith Williams. When starting his first pastoral call, to Casper, Wyoming, in 1944, Pastor Williams was recruited to help at Casper's Boys Club by a local youth—Jim Reeb. After high school graduation and two years in the U.S. Army, Reeb used his GI Bill rights to study at St. Olaf College. He chose the Northfield, Minnesota, school at the urging of Griff Williams, an Ole alumnus. Reeb then went to Princeton Seminary and was ordained into Presbyterian ministry. He later became ordained in the Unitarian-Universalist communion, because he valued its focus on social action. By the time Reeb and Williams were together in Selma, the latter was serving at Lutheran Church of the Master in Edina, Minnesota. (Williams completed his call there in 1986 and died in 2009.)

The Selma marches were planned for arrival at the state capitol in Montgomery, about sixty miles east. But the March 9 march, like one two days earlier, was stopped at a bridge departing Selma by attacking state police.

That evening Reeb dined at an integrated Selma restaurant with two other Unitarian-Universalist ministers. When leaving, they were attacked by white men, and Reeb was clubbed on the head. He died two days later. A month later three white men were indicted for Reeb's murder; all were acquitted in December.

A successful Selma to Montgomery march was accomplished later in March 1965. And Reeb's death provoked mourning nationwide. President Lyndon Johnson called Reeb's widow to express condolences, and on March 15 he invoked Reeb's memory when delivering the Voting Rights Act to Congress. Adopted in August 1965, that law has produced dramatic change in southern-states' voting participation by racial minorities.

Obviously, not all the church folk pursuing racial justice fifty years ago were Lutheran, but Lutherans were among them. And they shall live in a grateful nation's memory.

CHARLES P. LUTZ

August 1961: Martin Luther King and Lutherans Divided

August, for many Americans, will always be associated with the sainted Martin Luther King Jr. In August 1963 his "I Have a Dream" speech at Washington's Lincoln Memorial captivated millions. Exactly two years earlier, King addressed 14,000 young Lutherans at the first Luther League Convention of the American Lutheran Church (ALC).

Martin Luther King Jr. at the Lincoln Memorial

To many in the newly formed ALC, King wore no saintly aura. Several months earlier, when it was announced that he would speak to Lutheran youth in Miami Beach, Florida, the young Lutheran denomination was torn by division.

The nation first heard of King just five years earlier. A Baptist minister in Montgomery, Alabama, not yet twenty-seven years old, King emerged as leader of a bus boycott by African-Americans. (This writer heard about King when a recent graduate of the seminary I attended—Capital, now Trinity Lutheran, in Columbus, Ohio—came to tell us about Montgomery's protest movement. He was Bob Graetz, Montgomery's sole white clergyperson supporting the boycott.)

In the half-decade following the Montgomery action, King strode the national stage as leader of what became the Civil Rights Movement. It was a time of major social unrest, with the quest for racial justice and Martin Luther King Jr. leading the way. His work for racial integration was cloaked in controversy. To supporters, King was a prophetic reformer, a courageous churchman pursuing much-needed social change non-violently. To dissenters, he was at best a radical agitator, at worst a Communist infiltrator.

The ALC's eighteen regional bishops (then district presidents) met to discuss the churchly ferment. They weren't opposed to racial reconciliation, but they had deep concerns about division in the young church body. They agreed, unanimously: "for the peace of the church" the youth division should withdraw the King invitation.

Their urgent plea reached the ALC national office in Minneapolis. The national president, Fredrik Schiotz, told the youth board he disagreed with the district leaders and said the invitation for King to speak should stand. The youth board agreed.

Then, just months before the convention, Dr. King sent word of his withdrawal from the convention program. He had learned of the ALC distress and said he did not wish to be the cause of division in the church. King
L. David Brown

was now based in Atlanta, and the Rev. David Brown, ALC youth director, went to meet with him. Pastor Brown was able to persuade the civil rights leader to stay as a scheduled youth convention speaker.

But that didn't end the controversy. Some congregations decided their youth would not spend August 15-20 in Miami Beach. Enough did come

The 1961 Luther League Convention

King speaking at the convention

Martin Luther King Jr. as part of a panel addressing racial justice

to make the total of 14,000 Leaguers and accompanying adults the largest Lutheran youth assembly ever in North America to that point.

What did King tell them? The convention theme was "Christ Is Living," and King addressed "Christ Living in the World." He asked Luther Leaguers living in an unjust world to be "proudly maladjusted." He said the fundamental need for youth of the church is to share God's love when facing societal injustice.

King spoke on the convention's second day, Later that day he joined a panel addressing questions about racial justice. Among the panelists were: Bob Graetz, the white pastor who had worked with King in Montgomery; Pastor Joe Bash, a youth staffer; and Don Luther, a Luther Leaguer whom that convention elected to a three-year term as president. ALC unrest over the King invitation basically died once the convention was over. Controversy stirred by its youth division did not. The youth board, chaired by Pastor David Preus, who served at University Lutheran Church of Hope, Minneapolis, and later became ALC presiding bishop, believed—along with the youth staff—that God was calling them to provide prophetic leadership in the tumultuous 1960s on church/society agendas—not just for young people, but for the entire church!

CHARLES P. LUTZ

Women's Ordination

Among the powerful implications of Luther's preaching about divine grace is the recognition that every Christian is called to act as a little Christ in every life circumstance. However, social conventions long delayed full implementation for women's ministry within and on behalf of the church.

Sixteenth-century Lutheran reformers taught that no occupation or relationship has any more spiritual value than another, and all share in what has come to be called the priesthood of all believers. Baking bread is as honorable a work as consecrating that bread as the body of Christ; teaching a child to read a book is as honorable as preaching from the Bible.

This expansion of religious vocation beyond the pastor combined with rejection of monastic life and supported a spiritualized view of the home. A Christian woman's work as wife and mother was not second best; as a way in which she lived out her faith in service to 'neighbors," it was given religious meaning. Girls were offered basic education that allowed them to better understand Christian teaching and prepared them for their adult work. However, almost without exception, women were expected to answer their calling exclusively within the privacy of their own household. That their daughters, as well as their sons, might be called to the task of preaching the gospel and administering the sacraments did not occur to the reformers as a real possibility. The priesthood of all believers did not automatically open ordination to women. That reform came more than four centuries later.

As evangelical preaching spread in Europe, when Scandinavians and Germans migrated to North America, and as Lutheran missionaries carried the gospel around the globe, women answered their callings, most often within domestic boundaries. The revival of deaconess work in the 1830s gave women opportunities for more public service, particularly in health care and other works of love. In Pietist circles some women were lay preachers.

By the mid-twentieth century many American Lutheran women were assuming new roles: serving on their local church council, assisting in worship, and staffing church agencies as well as continuing to teach Sunday school, sing in the choir, and participate in women's organizations. Women's work was expanding, both inside and outside the church, but more quickly and more dramatically outside.

The second wave of American feminism was eroding assumptions about gender roles, breaking down old cultural boundaries, and questioning conventional restrictions on women's religious activities. In the late 1960s a few women enrolled in Lutheran seminaries. Their presence suggested the possibility that women who had the requisite gifts and training might be called to church ministries, not only as lay workers in congregations and on campuses, but as ordained pastors.

Already Lutheran churches in Scandinavia and Germany had begun to ordain women. Danish Lutherans were the first in 1948. Other American Protestant churches had done so even earlier. The time had come for American Lutherans to explore the full practical implications of Luther's expanded theology of vocation, specifically to investigate the qualifications for the pastoral office and opportunities for women to answer their callings within and on behalf of the church.

At the same time American Lutherans were exploring possibilities for closer relations between their churches and increased cooperation in their work. Although the major church bodies—the American Lutheran Church (ALC), the Lutheran Church in America (ALC), and the Lutheran Church–Missouri Synod (LCMS)—each considered the matter internally and would make independent decisions, scholars from all three carried out a joint study for the Lutheran Council in the U.S.A. (LCUSA).

Biblical, theological, ecumenical, and practical issues were taken up in several forums. A summary of the LCUSA study was widely distributed. Seminary faculty addressed the questions. Church leaders were surveyed for their thinking. Church members responded. Individual opinions, variously grounded, ranged from support to opposition.

Among women, as among men, opinions about the legitimacy and advisability of women's ordination varied. National women's organizations leaders were supportive, but some women were resistant or strongly opposed. Only a few women were included in official deliberations and the study process.

Three women were members of the LCA's Commission on the Comprehensive Study of the Doctrine of the Ministry. Historian Dr. Margaret

Sittler Ermath, a faculty member at Wittenberg University, contributed a position paper on women in the life of the church to the Commission. It was published as *Adam's Fractured Rib*. Texas Lutheran geology professor Evelyn Streng and American Lutheran Church Women officer Margaret Barth Wold were hastily appointed to the ALC's ad hoc committee when the lack of female representation was pointed out.

Many scholars within the LCA and ALC, perhaps most, agreed that neither the Bible nor the Lutheran Confessions provide a definitive answer. Therefore, the question would be resolved by "sanctified common sense." (The phrase is attributed to ALC President Fredrik A. Schiotz.) In contrast, influential leaders in the LCMS contended that the Bible prohibits women from exercising this public office. Their position highlighted fundamental disagreements about how to read and interpret the Bible and foreshadowed controversies to come.

Finally the decision to authorize women's ordination rested with the voting members of the churches' conventions. The question was not brought before the LCMS. In June 1970 the LCA convention passed the change; the ALC did the same in October. A half century after American women gained the right to vote and two years before Title IX guaranteed girls and women greater access to sports, the door to the pastoral office was opened to American Lutheran women.

Elizabeth Platz (above) was the first woman ordained in the Lutheran Church in America. Barbara Andrews (right) was ordained one month later in the American Lutheran Church.

Elizabeth Platz and Barbara Andrews, the first to enter that door, did so before Christmas. In the decades since hundreds of women have responded to God's call, using their talents and training to proclaim the gospel and serve their neighbors as ordained pastors in American Lutheran churches.

L. DEANE LAGERQUIST

Bread for the World: How Lutherans Have Led

The idea for what became Bread for the World emerged in the mind of a pastor at a small Lutheran Church–Missouri Synod congregation on Manhattan's Lower East Side. That pastor was Arthur Simon, and his idea evolved as Trinity Lutheran ministered among people living in poverty.

Trinity submitted a resolution on hunger to the LCMS national convention in July 1969. In response, the synod created a Commission on World Hunger. A few years later Simon co-authored a book, *The Politics of World Hunger*, with his brother Paul, then Illinois' lieutenant governor and later a U.S. senator from that state. Art remembers:

> After the manuscript was at the publisher, it occurred to me that political action by church members was the missing piece in the churches' response to hunger. . . . We organized first in the New York area, in March 1973, using the name Bread for the World.

A year later Bread for the World (BFW) began organizing nationwide and Simon became its first president. "Our goal from the outset was to get at the underlying causes of hunger and poverty through better government policies," says Simon, "and to do that intentionally as a response to the gospel.

Arthur Simon

An early question facing BWF's founders was its explicitly Christian identity. "We decided our task was to energize church people," Simon notes, "and explicit biblical content has always been central for us, though our approach to government leaders is always couched in secular policy language."

BFW's first legislative initiative was a "Right to Food" resolution, introduced in Congress in 1975 and adopted a year later. It says the

U.S. government "reaffirms the right of every person in this country and throughout the world to food and a nutritionally adequate diet." BFW had fewer than 10,000 members when "Right to Food" was adopted, but it was able to generate more than 100,000 letters to Congress on the issue. Many church members and others who are not formally BFW members do become involved in its work. By 2014 its membership had grown to more than 73,000, and its annual offering of letters now produces communications to Congress totaling in the hundreds of thousands.

Always focused on a specific legislative proposal addressing domestic or global hunger, the letters in many congregations are gathered, along with that week's financial gifts, at offering time during worship and later mailed to the respective U.S. representatives and senators. In other congregations, members receive background information on the legislative proposal and then respond individually. BFW's success in gaining congressional support for hunger-combating programs has been remarkable. Its campaign launched in the organizations fortieth anniversary year, 2014, was "to do our part to make hunger and poverty a national priority by 2017 and to help end hunger in our country and around the world by 2030."

Lutherans have been disproportionately supportive of BFW from its start. "Most Lutheran church bodies made annual grants from the very first," says Simon. "Martin Poch of the LCMS Board for World Relief was a strong supporter. But the most powerful early boost was an endorsement letter Presiding Bishop David Preus sent to all ALC pastors. It brought a great response: The ALC for years thereafter had twice as many Bread members as all other Lutherans combined."

Art Simon left BFW's presidency in 1991. Named to replace him was another LCMS-trained pastor, David Beckmann, who had served at the World Bank for fifteen years. Prior to joining the World Bank, Beckmann had worked in Bangladesh with Lutheran World Federation. Beckmann sees particular reasons for Lutherans wanting to combat hunger:

David Beckmann

We have lots of people with roots in farm country, and that has given our church a gut feeling for land and food concerns. Further, the gospel really does make a difference among us. We understand God's grace and want to show our gratitude by helping others. Lutherans like Bread also because we stay close to Bible language.

Beckmann adds:

For forty years Lutherans have focused strongly on hunger, more than any other U.S. church community. And Lutherans have always understood that the solution to hunger includes not just direct aid but also improving people's capacity to make a living, plus public-policy advocacy.

Since its birth, Bread for the World has been Lutheran in its leadership and grassroots membership. In 2014 it estimated that Lutherans comprised about twenty-five percent of its 73,000 members. ELCA Presiding Bishop Elizabeth Eaton spoke at the organization's 2014 anniversary celebration, saying that "Bread for the World is a ministry of the ELCA."

It's somewhat surprising that Lutherans, not known historically for political activism, have been leaders in the politics-of-hunger arena. Indeed, George Johnson, ALC Hunger Program coordinator in the 1980s, believes "it was concern about hunger that helped many Lutherans to get politically active for the first time, and from there they entered other social concerns as well."

CHARLES P. LUTZ

For Lutherans, the Quintessential "Family Reunion"

Ask a Lutheran what constitutes a "mixed marriage" and, more likely than not, they'll tell you it's the wedding between a Norwegian and a Swede, or a Dane and a German. It's a joke, but it wasn't always so.

When we think of the development—and consolidation—of Lutheran church bodies in North America, the mixed marriage metaphor doesn't quite work. The better image might be that of a family reunion. Lutherans came from Europe in great waves of immigration, over the space of 300 years. Because (unlike Anglicans/Episcopalians or Roman Catholics) Lutherans on this side of the Atlantic were not hierarchical, they had no bishops to tell them how to organize themselves.

The result was dozens (some historians suggest as many as 150) separate Lutheran church bodies, primarily in what became the United States. It was a natural result. Lutherans were separated by geography, language and ethnicity. The resulting hodge-podge of sometimes competing, sometimes overlapping church groups led to the comic-tragic saying, "Lutherans are a faith community divided by a common heritage."

The groups began combining by the early twentieth century. For the most part, Germans combined with other Germans, Norwegians with other Norwegians. (There was only one Swedish church, and the two Danish groups kept their distance from one another.)

By the mid-1960s there were only three large Lutheran church families left in the United States (along with some very small Norwegian groups that wanted to keep their independent status). The "new" American Lutheran Church (ALC) brought together a lot of Norwegians (the ELC and the Lutheran Free Church) and Germans (the old American Lutheran Church) and one of two Danish groups.

Shortly after the ALC came into being, the United Lutheran Church in America, representing most of the east coast Germans, combined with the (Swedish) Augustana Synod and the other Danish church to form the Lutheran Church in America (LCA).

The Lutheran Church–Missouri Synod (LCMS) was the third large group.

For a brief period during the 1960s there was a fond hope (not very realistic, as it turned out) that the Big Three would find a way to combine into a unified Lutheran Church for the country (if not for all of North America). One sign of that dream was the creation of a common worship book, the green-cover *Lutheran Book of Worship*.

But the brief window of hopeful optimism quickly closed. The Lutheran Church–

Missouri Synod rejected the hymnal their scholars helped to create (although some LCMS congregations began using it anyway). In the 1970s a conservative movement in the Missouri Synod guaranteed no significant cooperation was going to result between that church and the other two large U.S. Lutheran groups.

That didn't stop leaders of the ALC and the LCA from moving toward a new church body of their own. As early as 1980, the publishing houses of the two churches—the LCA's Parish Life Press and the ALC's Augsburg Publishing House—began developing and marketing common curriculum for Sunday schools, confirmation classes, and adult education.

In the 1980s four Lutheran seminaries combined into two. In Ohio, the LCA seminary in Springfield and the ALC seminary in Columbus joined to form Trinity Lutheran Seminary on the Columbus campus. In the Twin Cities, the LCA's Northwestern Seminary moved from Minneapolis to a site adjacent to the campus of Luther Seminary in St Paul and built a striking new academic complex. A few years later, the schools combined to become Luther-Northwestern Seminary (these days called simply Luther Seminary).

Increasingly, leaders and lay members of both the ALC and the LCA found fewer if any compelling reasons to remain separate. That led to the creation of the Consultation on Church Union, a task force that smoothed the way for a merger in 1988. The new church body, with over five million baptized members, borrowed the name of a previous Norwegian Lutheran body (the Evangelical Lutheran Church) and added the words "in America" to become the Evangelical Lu-

First officers of the ELCA: Vice President Christine Grumm, Presiding Bishop Herbert Chilstrom, Secretary Lowell Almen

theran Church in America. The new acronym became ELCA.

There was something striking about the creation of the ELCA. Unlike the all-German Wisconsin Evangelical Lutheran Synod or the almost-entirely-German Lutheran Church–Missouri Synod, or the several very small all-Norwegian Lutheran groups, the ELCA combined the ethnic heritages of a broad spectrum of European Lutheran heritage—German, Danish, Norwegian, Swedish, Finnish. It was the quintessential "Lutheran family reunion."

The ELCA is the largest Lutheran faith community in the western hemisphere (larger than the LCMS and more than ten times the size of WELS). The denomination is the most progressive (some would say "liberal") of all U.S. Lutheran bodies. Like any family, there are squabbles and disagreements. But, for the most part, the signs are that the members of this multi-national church family are glad they got together.

MICHAEL SHERER

Festival worship at the Constituting Convention of the ELCA, 1988, Columbus, Ohio

The Newest Lutheran Denominations: LCMC and NALC

For most of the twentieth century, Lutherans in North America were driven by the "urge to merge." In 1900 the Lutherans as a denominational family had grown in numbers to become the third largest Protestant group in the United States. But Lutherans were still divided into at least sixteen different denominations, separated mainly by ethnicity, language, and theology. While theology would still remain a dividing point, ethnicity and language declined as factors after World War I, with the end of immigration and the widespread transition to the use of English. "Now was the time," proponents said, "that Lutherans should all come together and join in a single denomination." The idea was that a unified Lutheran church would be more efficient and powerful, just like big government and big corporations. So in the twentieth century American Lutherans spent huge amounts of time and energy in merger negotiations. The dream of a single Lutheran denomination never happened, but by 1988 the vast majority (ninety-five percent) of Lutherans were members either of the Evangelical Lutheran Church in America (ELCA) or the Lutheran Church–Missouri Synod (LCMS).

But mergers have not generally brought about the benefits that their supporters envisioned. Often these mergers were engineered by minimizing points of dispute or leaving difficult decisions for the new denomination to solve further down the road. Such was the case with the merger that brought the ELCA together in 1988, uniting three Lutheran groups, each with a distinct ethos and organizational system. Difficulties abounded in the first years of the ELCA, compounded by "hot-button" issues, especially around ecumenical relations, the definition of the ministry, and human sexuality.

The first two of these problems, ecumenical relations and the nature of the ministry, were identified in the ELCA in the 1990s because of a movement to bring about closer relations between the ELCA and the Episcopal Church, including the interchangeability of clergy. This was not an easy task, because the Episcopal church is constituted by a distinct form of ministry, which is an essential and unchangeable part of their nature. They are a church built on bishops in the "historic episcopate," the historic transfer of legitimacy from one bishop to the next through ordination. The ELCA did not have this, so to gain ecumenical relations with the Episcopalians, they would have to conform their ministry system to theirs. A number of ELCA Lutherans objected to this, saying that this ran counter to the Lutheran understanding of the ministry. A resistance group, the Word Alone Network, was born in 1997 and continued to resist even after the ecumenical agreement with the Episcopalians was approved in 1999.

Some of those opposed decided that as a result of the 1999 agreement they could no longer stay in the ELCA. They met in 2001 to form a new Lutheran denomination which they called the Lutheran Congregations in Mission for Christ (LCMC). The word "congregation" in their title was an indication of their new theological approach; they hold that the local congregation is the center of power, and that while the new LCMC denomination is there to support and encourage the congregations in their mission, the denomination itself has no formal power over its congregations. The LCMC was trying a new approach to structuring Lutheranism in North America, not one unheard of, but rare.

The second issue to divide the ELCA was that of human sexuality, especially proposals to allow the ordination of non-celibate gay clergy. Though an earlier sexuality study in the ELCA was shut down after controversy, a second proposal to allow such ordinations was passed by the ELCA Churchwide Assembly in 2009. Opponents of this action met in 2010 and decided to form their own new denomination, the North American Lutheran Church (NALC). This group is organized along lines that are more traditional to American Lutheranism, but has a number of its own distinct features. The LCMC and NALC understand themselves as "centrist" Lutheran denominations; unlike the "conservative" LCMS they do ordain women, but they are not "liberal" like the ELCA.

In 2017 the LCMC consisted of over 350,000 members in 750 congregations in North America, while the NALC has 140,000 members and 400 congregations. Taken together, this represents the largest schism in American Lutheran history, at least since the 1860s, and a major portion of the membership decline in the ELCA, which has lost 1.3 million members since 2001. Advocates for the LCMC and NALC see the formation of these two groups as a positive sign, giving Lutherans new choices and options, and by doing so beginning to revitalize Lutheranism on this continent. They argue that more choice and more competition will actually be better for the long-term growth of Lutheranism in North America.

MARK GRANQUIST

Wittenberg Meets Addis Ababa: Lutherans in East Africa

There has been a huge and unprecedented shift in the geographical location of Christianity over the last 100 years. In 1900, two-thirds of all Christians lived in the North Atlantic world (Europe and North America). But by 2000, this percentage had shifted. Now two-thirds of all Christians live in the Global South (Latin America, Africa, and Asia). And while Christianity in North America is holding steady, and in Europe is declining, the growth of Christianity in the Global South is nothing short of explosive. The magnitude of this change is only beginning to be felt, but will be a major factor in Christianity in the twenty-first century.

This change is also true for Lutheranism, as four of the ten largest Lutheran populations are now in the Global South, and this is where Lutheranism is growing the fastest. The total numbers of Lutherans in Africa increased from 5.6 million in 1987 to 18.7 million in 2009. Three of largest of these rapidly growing Lutheran populations are in East Africa: Ethiopia (7.9 million), Tanzania (6.5 million), and Madagascar (3.0 million), which, along with Kenya (150,000), make up now one of the largest concentrations of Lutherans in the world. The work that Lutheran missionaries began in East Africa in the nineteenth and twentieth centuries was taken up and dramatically expanded by African Christians, to the point that there are now more Christians in East Africa than in North America.

Johan Ludwig Krapf

The first modern European missionaries tended to avoid Africa, with its difficult climate, in favor of work in Asia, especially India and China, begun in the eighteenth century. One of the first Lutheran missionaries to Africa was Johan Ludwig Krapf, a German working for the British Church Mission Society, who began a long pioneering mission in East Africa in 1837. Along with several other later missionaries from Germany, Krapf began to survey East Africa for mission stations, worked on reducing local languages to written form, and began to convert local people to Christianity. This initial work was difficult. Political considerations and the hostility of some groups made their work difficult, and diseases took their toll. When the British and Germans began to colonize East Africa in the late nineteenth century, more mission work became possible (though identification with the colonizers was not always a positive thing).

Mission work on Madagascar was begun by missionaries from the Norwegian Mission Society in 1866, as an extension of work they had already begun in South Africa, and expanded rapidly after that. The first Norwegian-American missionary arrived in 1887, and soon there was a flourishing mission in that country. The formal Lutheran presence in Ethiopia also began in 1866 with missionaries from the Swedish Mission Society, and later other European (and later American) Lutheran mission societies also came to work there.

NLCA missionary David Lovass teaching a class in Madagascar between 1916 and 1931

These groups had to work initially at the margins of the country, as the Ethiopian emperor sought to safeguard the territory of the Orthodox church in that country. In Tanzania, formal Lutheran mission work began in 1887, and, because the territory had just been colonized by Germany, the leading Lutheran mission groups in the country were German. Though there was much Lutheran mission traffic through Kenya, formal Lutheran work there was not begun until after World War II.

Mission work is always affected by political chang-

Missionary Viola Fischer with nurses, part of Augustana's mission to Tanganyika (now Tanzania)

Staff and student body at Onesimus Nesib Seminary, a regional seminary in Ethiopia, where the explosive growth of the church creates a great need for pastors

es, and this was especially true in East Africa. Pressure from indigenous leaders affected work in Madagascar and Ethiopia, and the Italian conquest of the latter country disrupted mission work for a time. World Wars I and II meant that European mission societies could not work in East Africa, and American Lutheran groups stepped in to support these "orphaned" missions, especially the Swedish and Swedish-American missionaries in Tanzania. With the formation of the Lutheran World Federation in 1948, this new body took over the job of coordinating much of the Lutheran missionary work in East Africa.

Though Western missionaries played an important role in the beginnings of Lutheranism in Africa, it must be said that the success of this work, and of its phenomenal growth, was due to the response of African Lutherans to the gospel, and to African church leaders, who have accomplished much of this work. Many missionaries realized early on that training African Christian leaders was the only way that Lutheranism would catch hold and flourish in East Africa, so Lutherans developed a number of seminaries and theological schools for the education of African Lutheran pastors and leaders. When many African countries became independent in the 1950s and 1960s, these local Lutheran leaders established, out of the mission congregations, their own independent Lutheran churches. Western missionaries still work in East Africa today at the invitation of these independent churches, mainly in areas of education and support. The future looks bright for East African Lutheranism, and Lutherans in North America are beginning to learn the faith in new ways from their Africans friends and colleagues.

MARK GRANQUIST

For Further Reading and Reference

Dictionaries

Timothy Wengert, ed., *Dictionary of Luther and the Lutheran Tradition*. Grand Rapids: Baker Book House, 2017. A forth-coming reference book which will be very useful and current.

Erwin L. Lueker, *Lutheran Cyclopedia*. St. Louis: Concordia Publishing House, 1975. A very useful single volume reference. Entries are not lengthy but can be very helpful for basic details. Also online as the "Christian Cyclopedia"—http://cyclopedia.lcms.org/

American Lutheran Histories—General

Mark A. Granquist, *Lutherans in America: A New History*. Minneapolis: Fortress Press, 2015. The most current and up-to-date general history.

E. Clifford Nelson, ed., *The Lutherans in North America*. Philadelphia: Fortress Press, 1975. The previous standard history on the subject, especially good on the institutional history.

Wentz, Abdel Ross, *A Basic History of Lutheranism in America*. Revised edition, Philadelphia: Fortress Press, 1964. Prior to Nelson the standard history, still very useful.

L. DeAne Lagerquist, *The Lutherans*. Westport Connecticut: Greenwood Press, 1999. An excellent interpretative history, though not as detailed as Nelson or Wentz.

American Lutheran Histories—Popular

Todd W. Nichol, *All These Lutherans: Three Paths Toward a New Lutheran Church*. Minneapolis: Augsburg Publishing House, 1986. Brief histories of the three groups that formed the Evangelical Lutheran Church in America in 1988.

Charles Lutz, ed., *Church Roots: Stories of the Nine Immigrant Groups That Became the American Lutheran Church*. Minneapolis: Augsburg Publishing House, 1985. Subtitle says it all.

Lutheranism—Introductions

Kathryn A. Kleinhans, ed. *Together by Grace: Introducing the Lutherans.* Minneapolis: Augsburg Fortress, 2016. A good, brief, introduction to Lutheran theology and history.

Conrad Bergendoff, *The Church of the Lutheran Reformation: A Historical Survey of Lutheranism.* St. Louis: Concordia Publishing House, 1967. A good, readable general history.

Acknowledgments

The idea for these materials began with Bob Hulteen, editor of the *Metro Lutheran* newspaper (Minnesota) in 2009. He conceived of a project entitled "Faithful and Reforming: Lutheranism Over 500 Years," and gathered a group of writers, headed by Mark Granquist, to accomplish this project. The idea was that there would be a column in the *Metro Lutheran* each monthly issue, examining one aspect of Lutheran history, especially Lutherans in North America. Beginning in December 2009, there would be ninety-five columns, culminating in October 2017.

Over the years this project won several national awards from the Associated Church Press. Unfortunately, the *Metro Lutheran* ceased publication in May 2014, when only fifty-four columns had been published.

But, as it had always been the idea to gather these columns into a book, it was decided, with the help of Karen Walhof of Lutheran University Press, Minneapolis, to continue this vision. Additional columns were written and collected, and the book was produced. This has been done with the permission of Bob Hulteen of the *Metro Lutheran* and the authors of the additional columns—many thanks to all.

Authors of the columns include Maria Erling, Susan Corey Everson, †Willis Gertner, Mark Granquist, Mary Jane Haemig, Bob Hulteen, John Isch, Tom Jacobson, Russell Kleckley, L. DeAne Lagerquist, Robert Lee, David Lumpp, Charles Lutz, Meg Madson, †Fran Monseth, Tara Mulder, Bill Schaeffer, Michael Sherer, and Susan Tjornehoj.